THE WHO

A BROKEN W

THE

WHOLE PERSON

IN A BROKEN WORLD

by Paul Tournier

TRANSLATED BY

JOHN AND HELEN DOBERSTEIN

1817

HARPER & ROW, PUBLISHERS, San Francisco
Cambridge, Hagerstown, New York, Philadelphia
London, Mexico City, São Paulo, Sydney

This book is a translation of *Désharmonie de la Vie Moderne*, Delachaux &
Niestlé S. A., Neuchâtel and Paris, 1947.

LC: 64-14377
ISBN: 0-06-068312-0

83 84 85 10 9 8 7 6 5 4 3 2

To our two sons,
Jean-Louis and Gabriel,
to the young generation,
whose pardon ours must beg
for bequeathing to it a world so sick,
I dedicate this book

Contents

I THE INNER CONFLICT OF MODERN MAN   1

II THE PRECEDENCE OF PERSONHOOD   36

III THE RIFT BETWEEN THE SPIRITUAL AND THE TEMPORAL   68

IV THE MYTH OF PROGRESS   96

V THE MYTH OF POWER   125

VI THE TASK OF THE CHURCH   144

NOTES: WORKS CITED   171

INDEX OF NAMES AND SUBJECTS   177

THE WHOLE PERSON IN

A BROKEN WORLD

CHAPTER I

The Inner Conflict
of Modern Man

IT IS NOT necessary to be a great scholar to see that our world today is not in good health. It is a broken world. Its ills are innumerable; it writhes in its pain. If it has passed the acute stage of its illness, it is still not cured. We get the clear impression that it is enjoying only a temporary remission. What is this disease from which it is suffering?

This is the question that confronts the doctor every day at the bedside of the sick. To enumerate the symptoms, to discern the mechanisms that cause them, to examine more closely the lesions of the organs most affected still does not constitute a diagnosis.

Many clear-sighted men in our day have attempted to formulate this diagnosis. Most of them do so with caution, without concealing from themselves the difficulty of such an attempt. Moreover, the diagnoses which they propose are sometimes contradictory, which only increases our perplexity. Nevertheless, their efforts are not altogether fruitless. They are searching, and, after all, one does not find without searching. For my part, I ally myself with them, and I do not do so as one who claims to have found. Like them, I too am a seeker.

When we are dealing with a "difficult case" we consult with a number of doctors. We make our examination together in order to arrive at a more precise diagnosis. Each one of us formulates the hypothesis that comes into his mind. Afterward we examine the patient again, discuss the case, and see whether the hypothesis accords with the established symptoms.

It is in this spirit that I write this book. I will submit to the reader the hypothesis which presents itself to me as I seek to understand the sickness of the modern world.

There is a crisis today in every one of our disciplines, a crisis in science, a crisis in medicine, a crisis in law. There is a political and economic crisis, a philosophical and religious crisis. There are specialists who would be able, far better than I, to name and describe each one of these crises, and many others besides.

I am neither a historian, a theologian, nor a sociologist. In my own profession I am the least specialized of all doctors. I am nothing more than an observer of man, the infinitely diverse and infinitely similar man who comes to me day after day to open his heart. And this is precisely the reason I write; because behind all these particular crises there is a crisis of modern man. We must seek to define it more precisely. Again I say, it is a difficult task, and therefore I have been in search of a clue.

This clue I have found in what Pascal wrote: "All the generations of men, following each other in the course of so many centuries must be considered as one man who continues always to subsist and is constantly learning." With Pascal, then, let us view the history of man as the history of a single life.

When a sick person comes to us we always ask him first about his childhood and his adolescence; we seek to understand his development.

The childhood of mankind is Antiquity. Our sick person was a child prodigy. Antiquity has all the characteristics of a child prodigy, who seems to be able effortlessly and spontaneously to discover the purest, the truest, and greatest treasures, especially in the realm of art and poetry and dreams, just as if complete masterpieces came gushing forth from his childlike, innocent soul.

Among the patients I have been caring for in recent years, I have seen several who had been child prodigies and now as adults seemed to be going through a crisis which was the more profound the more their present difficulties contrasted with the success of their childhood. I think of one of them who in his youth had known innumerable easy triumphs which he now mentally compared with the mediocrity of all that he was able to accomplish today. So great was his despair that he retreated into complete inactivity and was haunted by the thought of suicide.

Childhood, Antiquity, is the age of poetry.

Since then humanity has gone through the Middle Ages, which we may compare with the school age of man. Until he reaches the point of emerging independence sometime in adolescence, the child obediently learns everything he is taught. He believes all that he is told to believe. He accepts without argument the authority of his parents and his teachers. It is the age of conventional religion, the acceptance of the religion that is taught. In the same way men in the Middle Ages grew up in the thought system which their teacher, the church, imposed upon them. They accepted it uncritically, without even noticing—in this respect like a child—that this teacher was not without fault. This is the age when the child believes that those who instruct him know everything and are perfect. He takes them for gods and accepts the faith and the morals which they present to him. And even if he disobeys, he still does not question their authority.

Then one day comes the age of adolescence. A flood of new knowledge, the intoxication of learning, and the yearning for personal experience confront the adolescent with a thousand problems, which, so it seems to him, his parents escaped. He rises up against them; he revolts. He demands the right to think for himself and not in accord with a system of traditional thought, the right to follow his own opinions rather than the authority of others. He sits in judgment upon his parents and finds that they themselves do not practice the morals they inculcate in him. He argues about everything and exults when his parents confess that they have no answers to the insatiable questions he asks.

Can we not compare this crisis of adolescence to that which was set off by the Renaissance?

What characterizes the adolescent is the fact that this self-assertion is still entirely negative. He believes that he is free and to prove that he is free he does just the opposite of what he has hitherto done as a docile child. His liberty, however, is more a matter of talk and argument than of creative activity. Simply to say No consistently where hitherto one consistently said Yes is not to be free.

In the same way, since the Renaissance, mankind has taken the opposite view of the world from that which had been taught by Antiquity and the Middle Ages. For a spiritual, religious, and poetic view of the world it substituted a scientific, realistic, economic view. Like the adolescent it flung itself passionately into study and tumultuously into extreme and contradictory doctrines. It was a violent reaction to the claim of the late Middle Ages which had tried to confine all culture and all of life in a rigid, logical system, derived from faith.

Just as the young man in revolt accuses his parents, so the modern world sees in the church the great obstacle which prevented it from becoming itself, from freedom of thought. Thus Nietzsche wrote: "What was the greatest objection to existence hitherto? . . . God. . . ."

What also characterizes our young adolescent is disparagement. He disparages the values in which he was raised. He scoffs at his parents. He regards their moral and social conformism as hypocrisy. Here we think of Sartre, who is so characteristic of our age, who see everywhere nothing but comedy. "Look at this coffeehouse waiter," he writes, "he is playing the coffeehouse waiter." And above all it is the traditional values he denigrates. "For him," writes Gabriel Marcel,[1] "to be the father of a family is always and inevitably to be someone who is *playing* the father of a family." And this last emphasizes "the resentment that animates Sartre against everything we have in view when we speak of the 'social order' and probably of any order whatsoever."

Thus the world as Sartre sees it is exactly the same world that is seen by our young man in revolt, who denounces everything represented by the people he admired in his childhood and now feels a bitter resentment toward them.

We can thus compare the centuries man has lived since the Renaissance to the critical years of adolescence.

This crisis is necessary and normal. Before he attains adult maturity the young man must go through this time of storm and stress when he has to subject everything to question. The day will come when he will discover again many of the treasures of his childhood, when he will return to the faith in which he grew up and the principles which were inculcated in him. For they were true, and life sees to it that he rediscovers them. But then he will give them a quite personal turn; he will profess them as his own convictions, based upon his innermost experience. In psychology this is called integration.

But sometimes this integration is delayed and the crisis of adolescence takes on the proportions of an illness. The psychiatrists call the illness the "neurosis of defiance" (*névrose d'opposition*).

Something like this, it seems to me, has taken place in the development of human history. Some such diagnosis I propose to make with respect to our modern world. It is therefore important, before we pursue our examination of the modern world, that we define this concept of the "neurosis of defiance."

Dr. Alphonse Maeder of Zurich in his fine book *Ways to Psychic Health*[2] gives an account, with the exactitude which is characteristic of him, of such a case. I shall give a brief résumé of it here and I recommend that the reader consult the author's detailed account of it.

A high school principal sent to Dr. Maeder a seventeen-year-old student whose grave failures in school went hand in hand with a fault-finding attitude. This adolescent boy, whom the author calls Max, dreamed of nothing but jazz. He had stolen money from his father in order to cover the expenses of an orchestra to which he devoted his time instead of working. Max was very reserved with the doctor and answered his questions laconically. Nevertheless, he betrayed that he was in serious conflict with his father, and this explained his reserve; for he transferred to all authorities—and the doctor was an authority, as were his teachers—the defiant attitude he adopted toward his father.

However, thanks to the doctor's benevolent attitude, the young man relaxed a bit and explained his grievances against his father: he was deeply disillusioned with this father because he did not defend Max's mother when her parents-in-law criticized her unjustly; this was an act of cowardice which ruined his authority over his son.

The next day the doctor found Max more receptive. He had lost his arrogance. He freely confessed that he felt unhappy, that his failures worried him, that he felt incapable of changing his attitude, and regretted the disappointments he had caused his father. But when the doctor suggested that he express his regrets to his father, the young man bluntly refused. "Certainly you do not expect me to do the precise opposite of what I have been doing!" But, Max was dumfounded when Dr. Maeder replied, "You told me yesterday that you are a revolutionary. Is it not precisely a revolution to do the very opposite of what you had been doing?" Max left the doctor with a "Perhaps . . ."

When he was questioned about his faith, the young man said that he no longer believed in God, that in this regard he adopted an attitude of independence.

Then the doctor sought to see the father of the boy to prepare him for the projected interview between him and his son. Asked to visit him, the father came, and he too was very cautious and reserved. The doctor, however, asked him very bluntly whether he did not recognize his own responsibility in the troubled family situation. After the first shock, the father softened and his eyes grew moist. The ice was broken. He admitted his fault and declared that he was willing to talk things over frankly and completely with his son.

The conversation between Max and his father lasted four or five hours. The father followed the doctor's advice, treating his son very kindly and generously assuring him of his desire to help him and to allow him freedom to choose between his studies and his music. Max was bewildered and came back to see the doctor. Now that he felt free, he saw that his difficulties were within himself. He was "actually afraid of himself." Of his own accord he confessed that he had lied, that he felt remorse with regard to masturbation, and his "dirty" thoughts. He added that he had doubts about himself, because in spite of his efforts he never got anywhere.

The doctor then explained to him the immense role that the conflict with his father had played in his failures, that his defiant attitude toward his father had carried over into his revolt against the school and his conflict with his teachers and that finally he had become the victim of his own revolt. Indeed, it had caused his revolt against God, who is the supreme authority, but also the source of all true victory over oneself. "The basic condition of man is presented in the allegory of the return of the Prodigal Son."

Thus the conversation passed imperceptibly from the field of psychotherapy to that of pastoral care. As the doctor shared with Max his own religious experiences, he showed the boy how, in the presence of God and in submission to his will, one can accept oneself as one is, accept the hard struggle of life, accept one's sexuality and master it.

And Max set out on his new path with fervor: "Behind the almost cynical realism of his former attitude," adds the doctor, "there was hidden a genuine idealism which he openly affirms."

Now, why do we say that this is a neurosis and not simply a normal crisis of adolescence?

What distinguishes a neurosis in the first place is anxiety. Note how this young man, who at first was so sure of himself, shows even in the second interview that behind this façade of bravado he is hiding a deep anxiety. He confesses that he is dissatisfied with himself. The first task of the doctor is to help him to become aware of this secret discontent.

In the same way there is in modern man a muffled discontent with himself, a distress of which he is not always aware. He too poses both as an innocent man and as an accuser; he denounces the culprits and these may be his wife, the opposing party, or some neighboring state. But when we talk with him more intimately we soon see that under this flood of criticisms he is concealing an inner anxiety. And here again there comes to mind a saying of Sartre which is very typical of our time: "Man is anxiety."[3]

What further characterizes a neurosis is its sterility. The big dreams the boy has, and even the genuine interest in jazz, are merely compensations and escapes; they do not produce the fruit which they might produce and they do not deliver him from his anxiety. In the same way we find in the modern world some true values—elite, literary, artistic, spiritual—but which have somehow been thrown out of gear and do not play an effective role in the destiny of society.

What is more, the tragic thing about neurotics is that the very efforts they make to save themselves destroy them. We can observe this paradox every day among our patients. It is as if their illness drove them to cut the life-line to which they are suspended. If they have put all their confidence in someone, an impulse drives them to behave in the very way that will ruin this confidence. When they wish to open their hearts to those who are near to them and put an end to misunderstandings, they go about it in such a manner that the misunderstandings are multiplied and their loneliness is aggravated. If they try to pass an examination, they work at it so desperately and anxiously that they lose all composure and are simply confounded.

I find the same paradox in the modern world. The efforts it makes to save itself bring it to ruin. The efforts it makes to avert war pitch it into war. The efforts it makes to guarantee its material security disrupt the economy and increase its misery. The efforts it makes to penetrate the secrets of nature and capture its energy lead to the atomic bomb, which threatens to destroy everything it has built up in the course of the centuries. The efforts it makes to free man from social slavery plunge it into struggles which only increase his burdens.

In many respects can we not see in the crisis of Nazism the same kind of neurotic gesture, which actually precipitates its ruin by the very means it has chosen to escape it? "National socialism," writes Wilhelm Röpke,[4] "was in large part the German form of an international mental disease." In any case, it is interesting to note how much the Nazi adventure reminds us of certain disorders that are characteristic of adolescence, notably the escapade. The "escapist," Dr. René Allendy[5] tells us, throws himself headlong into the naïve realization of a project that fascinates him without worrying about what will happen afterward; he is beyond all reasoning. Recall also the statement made by Goebbels: "When we win, everybody will want to be our friend." Thus, as with our neurotics, it was the desire to be loved that impelled him to do the very things that stir up hatred.

This behavior which produces the opposite of what is desired is one of the specific characteristics of neurosis, giving it the appearance of a curse, a doom, a rushing into self-destruction, a demonic force. It was in view of the Buchenwald concentration camp that Jung the psychoanalyst recently revived the ancient biblical concept of demons.[6] André Malraux,[7] in a recent interview, also spoke of it in connection with the atom bomb. And we know what Paul Valéry said: "We other civilizations know now that we are mortal."[8] And the day after Bikini, André George added this comment: "Suddenly civilizations have become more mortal."[1]

This impression that the world is racing to its ruin does indeed evoke the idea of an unconscious impulse. Gabriel Marcel[1] writes concerning the work of Sartre that one "may ask oneself whether this philosophy does not turn us to the abysses into which the powers of self-destruction today threaten to plunge our unhappy breed."

For the final characteristic of neurosis is that it has its source in an unconscious inner conflict. "The neurotic," writes Jung,[9] "is sick because he is not conscious of his problems." We saw this clearly in the case cited by Dr. Maeder. The whole procedure of healing lay in the effort of the doctor to help his patient advance beyond his apparent problems to his true, inmost problem.

May it not be, then, that modern man too is suffering from an unconscious inner conflict; that he too is unconscious of his real problem? Is he not feverishly seeking to ward off the political and economic difficulties which he regards as the sole cause of his ills, without finding any relief? Does he not wish constantly to augment his power, develop his techniques, regiment the individual in order to increase his production, without putting an end to his anxiety, because his true problem lies elsewhere? In the end has he not driven out of his consciousness the true problem, the true cause of his torments, and is he not now projecting them upon everything he encounters?

Here we come back to what we said about the Renaissance. Abruptly humanity rejected that which it had hitherto allowed to guide it. It resolved to pay no more attention to any judgment of value, no longer to trust any metaphysical intuition, any poetic inspiration, any supernatural revelation, and to build its civilization solely upon material realities and objective knowledge. On the whole today it is apparently still very little concerned with philosophical, artistic, moral, and religious problems.

It lets the specialists debate about them in their holes and cor-
ners, as if these questions had no importance for its destiny.
This, it believes, is determined by economics, science, technology,
and politics.

But mankind has not been able wholly to suppress these problems of value and feeling. It has merely repressed them in its
unconscious. Dr. Jung has illuminated the extreme importance
of the collective unconscious of humanity in which slumbers
everything that animated its spirit in times past: the world of
symbol, poetry, truth, justice. If Freud discovered the animal
unconscious, the instinctive unconscious, Jung has studied the
spiritual unconscious, what Dr. Arnold Stocker[10] calls the higher
unconscious and which still exists in modern man, intact and
active, though he has no clear idea of it. "The religions . . . were
the schools of life," writes Dr. de Rougemont.[11] And Dr. Maeder[2]
writes, "There is no doubt that it is the great world religions that
have educated humanity."

A person is a neurotic when he has repressed something without having really eliminated it. Modern man thinks he has eliminated the world of values, the world of poetry, the world of
moral consciousness; but he has only repressed it and is suffering from it, exactly as Dr. Maeder's young patient realized that
the morality which in his eyes was embodied in his father, and
against which he was rebelling, actually brought him to the bottom of his own heart and that therefore he was really fighting
against himself.

An inner conflict—this is what a neurosis is.

"Every epoch," says Dr. Josef Gander,[12] "has its own typical
malady." The typical sickness of our epoch is neurosis. Many
doctors agree that more than half of their patients suffer from
it. And this is not accidental. The cause of it is that our materialistic and amoral civilization no longer answers the deepest needs
of the soul.

Pavlov's experiments upon animals have shown that neurosis
is tied up with a kind of spiritual irresolution, or as the psy-

chologists express it, with an ambivalence. The modern soul is
hesitant. The evolution of society since the Renaissance has
shattered the traditional framework and now man is bewildered,
tossed to and fro by contradictory doctrines. The world tells
him that feeling, faith, and philosophical truth are unimportant.
And this same man cherishes at the bottom of his heart a justified intuition that these problems are nevertheless important.
His thirst for love, his spiritual loneliness, his fear of death, the
riddle of evil, the mystery of God—he no longer speaks of these
things; he represses them, but still they haunt him. Dr. Stocker[10]
has given us this penetrating definition of neurosis: an inner
conflict between a false suggestion and a true intuition. A false
suggestion from the modern world and a true intuition of the
soul, which in reality yearns for something altogether different
from science, power, and material goods.

Modern man suffers from repression of conscience.

Let us now try to define this idea more precisely.

I am often asked what I think of the relation between sin and
sickness. The following outline seems to me to give a clear picture of it:

The son who loves his father is right and healthy.

The son who hates his father is not right, but healthy.

The son who loves and hates his father at the same time is
neurotic. Neurosis rests upon an inner contradiction.

This is what makes it possible for many doctors to say that
the neurotic son will be cured if he frees himself from his moral
scruples and hates his father with all his heart. Other doctors,
however, say that he will never be able to stifle completely his
ideal of love and can only be cured by abandoning his hatred.

In the same way, I believe that if humanity, since the Renaissance, had really been able to eliminate the spiritual, to "kill
God," as some have believed it has, it would probably be less
sick than it is today. I am not saying that it would be in the

truth and in righteousness, but it would not be divided in soul, it would not be ambivalent.

The collective man, of whom Pascal wrote, has rejected his childhood. He has rejected the moral criteria of the past and refused to recognize anything except the reason, the yardstick, and the scales. But the idea of the beautiful, the good, the just, his need for communion with his Creator, he has only been able to repress below the field of consciousness.

Freud saw nothing but the repression of instinct, and we know that for him the spiritual life and the conscience are based upon an illusion. Only the instinctive fear of losing the affection of his parents and society drives man to submit to the moral imperatives which they impose upon him. "One of the early psychoanalysts, Wilhelm Stekel," writes Dr. Maeder,[2] "went through an interesting development. . . . The many studies he published during the first twenty years of his activity are characterized by a strong emphasis on the instinctual aspects of behavior. As a genuine empiricist, in the course of time he learned many new things and came to recognize the moral law inherent in life. He finally arrived at a point in his development where he spoke of the psychoneuroses as illnesses of the conscience." Dr. Maeder goes on to say, "We now know that not repression of the instinct but also repression of the ideal, of the conscience, exists." He reminds us of all those men who "imagine that they have overcome religion," and yet who—as psychological analysis has revealed—are in reality dominated by an unconscious religious preoccupation. Their very aggressiveness against religion, such as that of many atheistic psychoanalysts, proceeds from this unconscious conflict. It is the projection of the hopeless struggle they wage within themselves to silence the voice of conscience and of faith. Here I can add my own testimony to that of my colleagues. Often I have been amazed to discover that the very men who most loudly professed their unbelief were in reality the most haunted by the spiritual problem, which they had not been able to eradicate. One of this kind, a Communist, came to me and said, "I hesitated because I know that you are a believer. I come on the condition that you will not speak to me about God." For a long time I compelled myself to observe the prohibition he had imposed upon me; but he talked about God the whole time!

According to Dr. Stocker,[10] Ernest Jolowicz was already saying of certain neurotic patients "that they have not resolved the transcendental problems, but only repressed them."

A French psychiatrist, Dr. Baruk,[13] chief of medicine in the Maison nationale de Charenton in Paris, has recently thrown great light upon this phenomenon of repression of the conscience and its consequences. In an exciting book he declares straightforwardly that he has "discovered on certain scientific, clinical, and experimental grounds the capital role of the conscience." This is by no means to be reduced, as the Freudians have asserted, to the psychic and mental functions of man; it is different from these. Dr. Baruk gives us the proof for this when he shows that in a maniac who is completely incoherent and demented in behavior an astonishingly vigorous moral personality with an acute sense of justice and of good and evil can persist." On the other hand, following Trélat, he describes *"les folies lucides"* (lucid insanity) and says: "The intelligence, the intellectual faculties appear to remain intact in these patients." This integrity is in contrast with a morbid alteration of the science, which in many respects is even more dangerous for society.

But whoever acts contrary to his conscience, Dr. Baruk goes on to say, "whoever violates the laws of equity and humanity exposes himself to feeling the effects of a very special illness. This illness consists in an intolerable inner judgment, so intolerable that very often it is immediately repressed by means of an extremely violent defense reaction which eliminates the intolerable feeling from the consciousness. But this elimination is only apparent and the disappearance of the guilt feeling is only an illusion: the feeling persists, camouflaged and unconscious, and therefore becomes all

the more redoubtable. When it ceases to express itself formally
in the inner psychology of the patient, then it expresses itself in
outward reactions which are incomprehensible in appearance and
often terrifying."

Another psychiatrist, Dr. Roger Reyss[14] says: "How many of
our patients are tormented by a feeling of guilt; how many exhibit upon analysis unresolved problems of life; how many have
systematized delusions. . . . I recall a patient of one of our teachers who 'in order to free herself of her guilt' made a real attempt
to construct a redeemer-myth, whereby, through a strange reversal, she discovered the impossibility and the vanity of human
effort. . . ."°

In order to justify himself, continues Dr. Baruk, the person
who represses his conscience "often tries to shift his discontent
upon innocent victims . . . and thus artificially creates culprits.
The weak are so well designed to play this role of scapegoat and
since they are innocent one must harass them all the more and
stir up hatred against them. . . . This is the mechanism of the
scapegoat, which has played an incomparably more important
role in social history and the history of nations than the aggressive instinct."

Thus, beginning with the observation of the mentally ill, Dr.
Baruk is able to show that the aggressive impulse and the conflicts which have stained humanity with blood proceed from a
repression of the conscience. They serve as a cover-up for man's
bad conscience. And here a man of letters joins the doctor: "The
drama of Europe," writes André Malraux, "is the drama of a bad
conscience."

Why is it, then, that science, which has studied man minutely,
for centuries has remained blind to such utterly important phenomena? The answer is that ever since Descartes it has imposed
upon itself an absolute prejudice: it refused any longer to take
into account spiritual and moral realities.

° A "strange reversal" because earlier, when she was in her right mind,
she had believed in the redemptive power of her own efforts. (Trans.)

This is in large part the fault of Christians. In the name of spiritual and moral values men have committed the worst atrocities. "These horrors," writes Dr. Baruk, "reached their peak at the end of the Middle Ages." And he quotes Jean Étienne Esquirol: "Everywhere they looked they saw only the excommunicate, the damned, and the witches. They were terrified, they created tribunals, the Devil was summoned, the possessed were hauled to judgment, gallows were erected, stakes were kindled. The demoniacs, who were called witches and possessed, doubly victims of the prevailing erroneous doctrines, were burned after torture to make them renounce their alleged pact with the Devil."

Alas, not only the sick were thus persecuted, but men like Galileo. . . .

We know how deeply affected a man like Descartes was by the fate of Galileo. When he saw how metaphysical and religious controversies set men against one another he conceived the plan of restoring accord by resolutely discarding all moral judgments of value. He therefore elevated to sole validity the criteria of reason, "common sense," and the measures of weight, length, and time, which nobody could argue about.

Disgusted by the abuses to which it led, humanity repressed Christianity by which it had so long been dominated. Repressed, but not eliminated. Herein lies, I believe, the essence of the tragedy of modern times. The modern man lives as if Christianity were a negligible hypothesis with no relation to the concrete realities of the world and society. And yet at the bottom of his heart this man remains impregnated with Christianity, so that he lives in a state of perpetual ambivalence with regard to it.

I shall now illustrate this with a series of practical examples.

Mr. So-and-so proclaims that the sole law of life is to get ahead and succeed. It is impossible to be honest in business; he has no scruples about cheating the public treasury or his competitors. But when he comes home and catches his son in a lie, he severely rebukes him: "I can forgive anything," he says, "but not a lie.

You should know absolute honesty is the sacred principle which no honorable man dare violate."

Ambivalence! Along with the whole of modern society he affects to believe that honesty, which is required by Christian morality, is inapplicable in the life of society. Yet he preserves the ideal at the bottom of his heart and clearly shows that he does so when it comes to the education of his child.

Ambivalence and uneasiness: he remains aloof from the church because he has a bad conscience, despite all the doctrines which he professes. He is afraid that he will appear to be a hypocrite—again a Christian idea!—if he is seen in church by his fellows, those who know very well that he tells lies in business affairs.

Several years ago I was asked to give an address on the theme: "Why do more women than men attend church?" At that time I made inquiries in many different places. And it is now clear to me that the reason for this lies essentially in the uneasy conscience. It impels a man to act, while a woman remains on the level of feeling. The sins of action are manifest, whereas those of feeling are generally unconscious. The man who is dishonest in business cannot go to church, cannot hear the law of the gospel, without feeling discomfort. A woman, on the other hand, who is jealous or who detests her daughter-in-law, can listen to and even approve a sermon on love without any feeling of embarrassment whatsoever.

Let it be understood that this description is much too schematic! I say this in order not to offend my women readers! I, who am a man, discover in myself, every day, sins of which I have been unconscious. And there are many women who have a more sensitive conscience than I do. Nevertheless, the fact remains that, if there are more women than men in our churches, the reason for this lies above all in the moral uneasiness of the men; entangled in social morals which are contrary to Christianity, they nevertheless remain secretly attached to it. "Have we sufficiently noted," writes the Rev. Ch. Durand-Pallot,[15] "from which social circles the great majority of Protestant churchgoers is recruited?

People with private means, functionaries, employees with fixed salaries. . . . How do we explain this selection? In great part by the following fact: the administrative employee, the school teacher, etc. are protected from that whole category of temptations which fall pitilessly upon all those who have to toil and resort to ruses to gain a place in the sun and keep it."

Another example: a married man deceives his wife. He loudly proclaims to all his friends that he has shaken off all false scruples in this regard, that the Christian ideal of purity belongs in the limbo of prejudices, that the condemnation of adultery has led to some dangerous repressions. He repeats what Sacha Guitry said: "Man is polygamous, woman is monogamous; all evil stems from this." What can he do? This is the way he is. If his wife reproaches him, he goes on the offensive with an aggressiveness that reminds us of Dr. Baruk's words.

But when it comes to his own daughter he is very much concerned about her conduct, and her acquaintances; he is very much afraid that she will "go wrong"—a phrase which in his mind relates only to sexual morality. He is so unnerved by his suspicions that he instills in his daughter the very fear of sexuality which he accuses the church of having disseminated in the world.

Or here is another who unduly practices birth control and down in his heart feels remorse because of it. "You can be certain," writes Durand-Pallot, "that if the listeners in our churches are made up so largely of aged people, the cause of it lies in this fact which I have mentioned."[15]

Why do so many of our best men, despite their concern for public welfare, stay out of politics? Because the man who enters into public life impelled by social idealism is soon so involved in the machinery that he no longer hesitates to compromise with his conscience. To justify himself he repeats to everybody the platitude that politics is the art of compromise and one must take account of realities. Ambivalence and uneasiness! In order to escape this uneasiness people stay out of politics. And those who most stoutly profess the doctrine of *"Realpolitik,"* how vehemently they denounce the bargainings to which their political adversaries descend! They retain at the bottom of their hearts an ideal of honesty and justice which they have received from Christianity, even though they declare that Christianity is outworn.

Jean-Paul Sartre, with his militant and consistent atheism, at least renders us the service of illuminating the strange contradiction of our present political world. A typical representative of the prevailing "laicism," M. F. Buisson,[8] has written: "We have become familiar with the idea that a people can live without religion. We have been working for thirty years to give increasing vigor to this idea." And now Sartre[3] cites the celebrated words of Dostoevski: "If God did not exist, everything would be permitted." He makes fun of "a certain type of secular moralism which seeks to suppress God at the least possible expense . . . ," the secular moralism which says, "God is a useless and costly hypothesis, so we will do without it." "And yet it is essential that certain values should be taken seriously . . . to be honest, not to lie, not to beat one's wife, to bring up children and so forth."

Yes, this "laicist" world, which so hotly badgers the church, preserves at the bottom of its soul a certain number of ideas which it has received from this very church.

But Sartre himself wishes to be more logical. He declares that, since there is no God, there are no normative values to which we can appeal; that there is neither good nor evil; and that there is no morality in the world that can prescribe for man one kind of behavior rather than another. And yet this same Sartre is constantly appealing in his argument to the "good faith" of his reader! Where did he get this value called good faith?

Let us look at the problem of law. One arrives, writes Professor Kaegi,[16] "at the negation of the idea of law" by way of the "process of the progressive secularization of the idea of law as a consequence of the general secularization of culture." As a matter of fact, in modern times the law has become a "formal law," a purely technical matter. It has divorced itself from its divine and moral origin. The judge must disregard his "subjective" conscience. He is simply bound to the law, which he must apply with the mechanical impersonality of a technician. He does not pronounce upon what is just, but merely upon what conforms with the statutes.

But when the German judges, bound by this modern conception of justice, began to apply the "racial laws" which had been promulgated by an anti-Christian regime, there were protests from all sides. Protests in whose name? In the name of an ideal of living, divine equity, which men no longer publicly professed, but which was preserved at the bottom of men's hearts, a sense of justice which came from a Christianity disavowed.

Or take the example of respect for human personality. "We Marxists," writes the Soviet historian, Pokrovsky,[1] "do not see in the personality the creator of history, because in our eyes the personality is only an instrument with which history works. The time will come when we shall be able to produce this instrument artificially, exactly as we produce our electric accumulators today." This comparison of man to a thing was not originated by Communism. It was done by capitalism long before. But what is the argument that both sides fling at each other if it is not the demand that the human personality be respected, a demand that has no other source except the Christian faith. When workers are exploited by capitalists as mere instruments of production, when Communists regard man as a mere instrument of history, when human beings are used as guinea pigs in concentration camps, in whose name do we protest, if not in the name of a Christian conception of man?

All modern materialistic medicine compares man with the animal. It sees in him merely "an aggregate of several trillions of cells, each one of which represents an assemblage of different molecules, and ultimately . . . electrons,"[17] which have been joined together by accident. And these doctors who deny that man is a spiritual being and recognize no ideal except the progress of science, are outraged by the fact that certain of their colleagues practice euthanasia or lend themselves as instruments of extermination camps. The point is that despite their materialistic theories they still preserve a conception of man which they owe to the very Christianity that they are criticizing.

Or look at the problem of marriage. Today we meet many men and women who profess a doctrine of marriage which is completely opposed to that of Christianity: free association between two independent beings. They refuse to make any concessions, they want to live their lives without having the marriage bond impose any limit whatsoever upon them. But look at the vehemence with which they denounce the selfishness of their spouses! But more, in the privacy of the office, in the course of psychological analysis we discover in them a secret and desperate yearning for a true marriage, for a real marital fellowship. In the end they confess that, like the fox who feigned indifference to the inaccessible grapes, they withdrew into their insistent independence only out of spite because they had not been able to achieve with their wives the deep unity for which they yearned. And when it comes to adultery, they confess to us that it was a thirst for a fellowship, a total self-giving, which they had not found in marriage, that drove them to it. So these too have preserved an ideal of marriage that comes from the Christianity which they apparently disavow.

Thus it appears to me that man today is suffering from an inner, more or less unconscious, conflict. I hope that I have shown this through these various examples. This inner conflict is undoubtedly the deeper source of the nervousness which is so common today and of those countless individual and social reactions which in their turn are increasingly poisoning the atmosphere of the family, the state, and international relations.

I have emphasized the unconscious character of this inner conflict because this is where the illness lies. It must not be confused with the eternal moral struggle which man cannot escape, and which St. Paul describes in the Epistle to the Romans. What characterizes modern man, as we have seen in the examples cited, is that he disregards the voice of conscience which is tormenting him inwardly. He thinks he has silenced it. He thinks he has promulgated a new morality. Thus his conflict is unconscious; it is a sickness, a dramatic struggle which destroys his personhood. Conscious moral struggle, on the contrary, the struggle with sin in the name of a consciously recognized law, is constructive, even though man may have his defeats.

This modern man adheres by turns to the most contradictory new doctrines—individualism, totalitarianism, Nietzscheanism, existentialism, scientism, or Freudianism. He regulates his conduct in accord with them; but at the bottom of his soul he preserves an ideal and a conception of life which he owes to Christianity: the idea of a divine law, qualms of conscience when he violates it, fear of punishment, the need for pardon, grace, and reconciliation with God and man, the yearning for a complete renewal of his being, and at the same time for personal fulfillment and fellowship with others. Indeed, he has received all these ideas from God himself through the teaching of the church; and therefore he cannot erase them from his consciousness.

The savant may pretend that he is free from all metaphysical prejudice and that he regards as negligible the imponderable facts of the moral and spiritual order; the sick person may demand of the doctor only a drug for his sleeplessness or a psychological prescription for social success; the doctor may confine himself as severely as he pleases to his technical and impersonal role: they all bear within themselves the confused feeling that neither the progress of objective knowledge, nor any medicine, nor any external success can free them from their profound anxiety, from their moral guilt, from their spiritual destiny.

They no longer talk about these things—the modern world has agreed to disregard them—but they suspect that this anxiety lies behind their physical, psychic, and social ills. They no longer speak of them, but they think about them secretly.

Dr. Jung has said that in psychological analysis every person over thirty-five years of age avers unconsciously or consciously that he is dominated by the fear of death and the religious problem.

Many of my colleagues say to me: "Of course I agree with you that the real torment of our patients is not that about which they talk to us. And this torment becomes a hindrance to the healing forces which we seek to arouse within them. But I do not know how to broach with them this essential subject of faith." The truth is that these doctors are themselves under the sway of that modern convention by virtue of which one conceals one's innermost preoccupations. They are afraid to overstep the strict limits of objectivity which science imposes upon their profession to penetrate terrain that is reputed to be taboo. Just like their patients, they pretend to live in a world all of whose ills have their origin solely outside of man: in microbes, in their wives, or in the government. As soon as they look at themselves as they really are, with their fundamental inner misery, they will find that their patients too will open up and talk about what is troubling their lives on the inside. As soon as they find the cure for their own inner confusion and the harmony which God restores in man when he returns to obedience to Him, they will be able to help their patients to experience the same thing. "No sooner does a man expel God from himself," writes Gustave Thibon,[18] "than everything within him (every fragment of his dislocated being) is successively summoned to become God; and at the same time to become war."

Undoubtedly it is because of the desire to free himself from this inner malaise that the modern artist has set for himself the ideal of sincerity. Everything is permitted to him as long as he is sincere. We have an example of this in Gide (which we shall discuss later) that shows how inappropriate is this way out for resolving the inner conflict. "It is not enough," writes René Gillouin,[19] "that a writer be sincere; he must be true. But on that high plane where genuine art moves, the true can no more be separated from the good than from the beautiful."

There also can be no doubt that it was to escape this inner malaise that man fabricated, following Rousseau, Nietzsche, Marx, or Freud, the doctrines which he vainly expects will free him from his guilt feelings. "That nobody can any longer be held responsible . . . this at last is the great liberation," proclaimed Nietzsche. And Sartre says, "We are unable ever to choose the worse."

"Many moderns . . . ," writes Dr. Maeder,[2] "explain the guilt feelings away and seek to consider them as mere ballast. Either they make light of them or are resigned to them. 'What do you expect? That's how it is. There is nothing you can do. Do not spoil your life because of it.'" And then he adds, "I ask myself how a physician who takes such an approach toward this essential question can help his patients." And Dr. Baruk[13] shows us that in the sick when this guilt feeling is repressed it only becomes the more injurious, that it constitutes the hidden source of their aggressiveness, their delirium, and their conflicts. This author does not hesitate to extend to the whole of society the mechanism which Dr. Maeder observed in his young neurotic. Modern man struggles in secret with his feeling of guilt. And there lies the true cause of the conflicts that rend society.

Here too lies the cause of a phenomenon which anyone can observe: our modern world is a world without conviction. Look at politics, economics, art, medicine. Everywhere men are improvising, dealing only with the most pressing matters. In the face of the urgency of the evils, men hastily seize upon superficial and often contradictory measures which merely aggravate the confusion. Ask these men the simplest questions about the real meaning of politics, economics, law, art, or medicine, the meaning and goal of life, culture, or the social order, and you will be astonished at their embarrassment. "Culture," says Malraux,[7] "must transform itself and yet it does not know where it is going."

In every one of us today there is a deep uncertainty that stems from our inner conflict, from that separation between our spiritual and our technological life.

The result is a world which is afraid. Without God, fear rules: fear with its two sets of reactions, the strong ones, such as bravado, aggressiveness, injustice, and the weak, such as panic, cowardice, and flight. The result is universal war. We know that science owes its upswing in large part to man's desire to escape from fear. To master nature, to understand in order not to have to fear any longer, to banish all mystery, this is what science has been striving to do. Listen, then, to this statement made by a man of science who stands in the front rank of this great movement, Harold Urey, Nobel prize winner and one of the physicists whose work led to the atom bomb: "I write to make you afraid. I myself am a man who is afraid. All the wise men I know are afraid."[1]

Now let us enlarge this idea of the repression of conscience and return to that collective and everlasting man, of whom Pascal spoke, and to that crisis of adolescence represented by the Renaissance. Not only did he throw overboard the law of good and evil, but also all the norms of his childhood, the whole world of the spirit, not only what we mean by "morality" but also by "philosophy," "religion," and "poetry," everything traditionally called "values" and so called even by those who, like Freud and Sartre, dispute them.

Even before the end of the Middle Ages there certainly were immoral men, contradictory philosophies, religious wars, and men whose minds were closed to all poetry. But nobody disputed the primary importance of these values, nobody denied their essential function in human nature. "An imperative which is addressed to the whole world," wrote Henri Bergson,[20] "already presents itself to us a little like a law of nature."

In the modern scientific age, nature appears as something completely different. Now it is viewed exclusively from the phenomenological angle, as a mere play of forces, of weights, size, and time, in short, of measurable, objective, quantitative facts. Science has its law within itself, it forbids itself all judgments of value, it closes its eyes to the qualitative aspect of things, it repudiates everything that proceeds from a subjective point of view. It takes an attitude which is the exact opposite from that of Montaigne. "The value of science," writes Emile Bréhier,[21] "issues from man who masters it and employs it. This is why, for Montaigne, man as he finds him in himself, is the perpetual subject of study."

The confusion appears especially in medicine: man is nothing more than the course of chemico-physical processes. The examination of the patient and contact with him are secondary considerations; the diagnosis is derived from an electrical recording apparatus or a chemical analysis in the laboratory. Numbers rule supreme. How novel it is to hear what Dr. Noël Fiessinger, the Paris clinician, recently said: "When mathematics enters into medicine, it should do so on tiptoe."[22] Along with him, many doctors of our time regard the primacy of the laboratory as an intellectual retrogression, when, after all, it was not so long ago that science seemed to confirm the triumph of the human intellect. To proclaim the autonomy of reason, to claim that it must be freed from all qualitative values, is to deny it. "Values lie at the base of the rational act of judgment," writes Arnold Reymond. Reason detached from values is nothing more than criticism, the criticism which was so dear to Renan, the doctrinaire of science.

Even we ourselves, who are seeking to react against this false view of the world, are still saturated with the prejudice which science has inculcated in us. We still have a repugnance toward grounding our conception of man upon what religion or philosophy tell us about him, toward attributing to metaphysical knowledge a value superior or even only equal to scientific knowledge. We still go on saying, "No need to discuss tastes and colors."

Next the repression of philosophy. Listen to the contemptuous tone with which many of our colleagues cry out when we speak of the spiritual aspect of man: "But that is philosophy!" The curriculum of medical study is very revealing in this regard. The future doctor, who must later face day after day the whole man, who will be called upon to understand him and his most intimate reactions and to counsel him with regard to his conduct, this future physician learns at the university nothing more about man than his anatomy and his physiology. Even of his psychology he knows only something about the brain centers and the reflexes which man has in common with the animals.

If one of our professors, an experienced clinician, permits himself a digression concerning the patient's life problems and spiritual difficulties, he knows that he is committing an extravagance, an offense against the principle upon which the faculty is founded: no philosophy! Happily there are some such professors, and their personal example alone does prepare the student a little for his future humane mission or at least causes him to think. But how gingerly and incidentally they must bring it in! For if they stress it, they expose themselves to the reproach that they are deviating from their role as men of science, that they are "philosophizing," "descending to the level of literature," or making religious propaganda. The university cannot officially concern itself with the philosophical and moral ideas of the students, even if this means that they may be led into cynical commercialism or mislead their patients into adultery or divorce.

Cannot one say the same about the study of law or theology? It seems to me that this extraordinary lack of philosophy in the modern university is less evident in France than in Switzerland. And yet a master of French medical science, Dr. Arnault Tzanck[23] says: "My whole life long I have sought for what my school instruction did not give to me. Philosophy is not merely something transcendent, a 'critique of pure reason' intended only for the initiate. . . . It can quite as well be summed up in the question which Montaigne posed for himself and which the most ordi-

nary person as well as the greatest savant asks himself: 'Who
am I?' "

True, there are still some philosophers. But we act as if they
were harmless specialists, who are allowed to go on discussing
forever things about which there will never be any agreement
and which have no importance for real life. As if the data of
science were not constantly being called into question after
having been universally recognized! It is pure prejudice on the
part of the modern world to assert that "values," ethical, religious,
and philosophical concepts are more uncertain and more arbitrary
than those of science.

Since Kant, men have distrusted metaphysical knowledge above
all. Our medical men claim that they indulge in no metaphysics
whatsoever. In reality, however, though they do not suspect it,
their whole thought is implicitly attached to a metaphysic. They
have an unconscious metaphysic; again a case of repression! Look
at the youngest of our medical disciplines, psychology, and the
pride with which, as Ribot[24] says, it has turned from "metaphysical psychology" and become a "biological psychology," that is
to say, a purely animal psychology!

The result is that appreciation of general ideas and genuine
intellectual thought is declining in the medical profession; specialization is making technological automatons out of physicians.
The more this indispensable specialization progresses, the more
necessary does it become that the physician be intellectually and
philosophically educated. "Whether he wishes or not," writes Dr.
Henri Mentha,[25] "the doctor is obliged to take sides. His counsels
will necessarily be inspired by an ethic, which, moreover, may
not necessarily be his own. He counsels divorce or patience—forgiveness or separation—family life or solitude—diversion or sub-
limation."

"Psychotherapy," writes Professor Viktor von Weizsäcker,[26]
"has, without knowing it, shown us that sickness is not to be
evaluated merely objectively according to a social and economic
scale, such as that of capacity for work, nor according to the

subjective standard of a conscious desire, like the desire for pleasure or gratification, but rather that sickness rests upon a certain profound reality, by virtue of which health has something to do with truth and suffering something to do with the negation of truth."

The University of Geneva has charged one professor of each faculty to take turns presenting to the whole student body the problem of truth and man. Such a beginning appears to be almost revolutionary today. For the university, which was founded to teach the truth, had forgotten to ask itself what truth is, whether there is such a thing and not merely partial and particular truths for each discipline and each specialization.

With the repression of the spirit, the university has lost its unity. In the various faculties men treat each other with deference and courtesy and all of them appeal to science as their authority; but there is no longer any genuine dialogue between medical men and theologians, between jurists and men of letters, between economists and artists. What once bound culture together in a unity was philosophy.

Then the repression of poetry. "We live," writes Dr. Alexis Carrel,[27] "in two different worlds, the world of facts and the world of symbols." Now the world of facts has the sole freedom of the city. Modern man has lost the sense of the symbol; he has repressed the symbol in his unconscious. We are reduced to the study of his dreams in order to recover it. It was not always so. In the past, poetry, music, and mythology nourished his soul and contributed to its development not less than mathematics. They spoke to it in their own intuitive language, which science cannot speak. And the modern soul suffers, despite the radio and the cinema, from artistic undernourishment. Art itself has abandoned the symbol in favor of realism. Certain painters operate purely with the reason and certain works of music imitate the sound of moving locomotives.

Modern man rejects the myths and symbols, because he sees

in them a naïve and outworn explanation of the world. Mythology, however, did not by any means claim to be an explanation of the world. This is a modern preoccupation. Mythology evokes realities which logical thought will never be able to express, realities which bring to the spirit a nourishment which is singularly richer than the demonstrations of science.

"Jean Piaget," writes Dr. Ferrière,[28] "has shown the considerable role that symbolism plays in the child. . . . People in the infancy of their culture make use of symbols as much as or even more than children themselves." If we reflect upon this hunger for symbols in the child, this yearning for poetry, we understand why it is that the modern school, which is directed wholly toward the world of facts (even in literature, which has become nothing more than philology), corresponds rather poorly to the child's real needs; and also very poorly to the needs of the masses of people who, though they are filled with popularized knowledge, have a secret nostalgia for that which would set their souls to vibrating.

True, there are still poets and artists, but, like the philosophers, they stand outside of society. Poetry is relegated to the role of a means of diversion. Children are no longer told the legends that are filled with eternal truths; they are given "factual instruction" on how oil is extracted from the earth. Children are no longer required to learn poems by heart; they are taught the history of literature. And at night they read the poets, in secret. And yet man's need for the mysterious is so great that we now are seeing the trashy symbols replacing the ancient symbols. We no longer speak of the Christmas angels singing to the wondering shepherds; we talk about Christmas trees and Santa Claus. And this humanity which believes that it has outgrown the age of naïve credulity swallows journals of astrology and acclaims the heroes of sport or the dictators.

It was philosophy, we said, that gave to culture its unity. In the same way, it was poetry that gave to men their unity. "There have been some civilizations," writes Pierre Hervé,[1] "without any connection with each other. . . . If the destiny of humanity to-day is to be one, if the tendency is toward the formation of one universal human nature . . . then the reason for this is that the whole of civilization on earth is growing toward unity." Not at all! Never will the fact that the same tractor is used on the steppes of Russia and the pampas of Argentina give to men the sense that they are one. This is something totally different. In his book *Le symbolisme des contes de fées* Leia[29] has shown that the same symbols are found in the legends of India, Finland, or of the Incas. These civilizations "without any connection with each other" therefore had a bond, a common spiritual bond, and this marks men of all times and all places with an inner seal and makes them brothers. "The stories and fables," writes Dr. Jean de Rougemont,[11] "served to educate the spirit, which today is singularly neglected." At the end of his book Leia shows that millenniums before Christ the cross appeared as a symbol of the encounter of the divine and the human.

Through the repression of symbols, the repression of art, the language of its unity, humanity has lost the sense of this oneness, and it suffers from this loss. Symbols are found in man's unconscious, but his rational civilization no longer responds to them. There can be no doubt that a civilization in which art has recovered its proper place will contribute far more than all the petroleum in the world to restore to broken humanity its solidarity.

A true work of art comes into being only where a bond of spiritual communion is established between the artist and his public, a bond which rests upon the resonances of their common unconscious. Why is it that a painting is more than a photograph, a sculpture more than its model, a symphony more than an assemblage of sounds, a book more than a dialectical puzzle of ideas, a drama more than a dialogue? It is because they awaken unconscious resonances. The spectators in the hall or theater are fully aware of this. Their emotion is no longer individual but collective; it creates between them an undefinable unity, because it awakens in them that which binds them together, namely, their unconscious, symbolic, poetic life.

Conscious ideas always divide men and set them in opposition to each other. On the conscious plane there are only arguments and conflicts. What brings men closer to one another is not only emotions but unconscious ideas, those of either the lower or the higher unconscious. One can give structure to a crowd of people either by mobilizing their instincts, their feelings of hatred and fear, or by awakening their spirit, their sense of beauty and love. A piece of Grand Guignol is just as effective in this respect as a mystery play. And men have such a great need for communion that when a civilization deprives them of this higher, spiritual unity they plunge into passions which unite them on a low level.

I have treated many artists. There are among them many neurotics, so many that one finally comes to believe that one cannot be an artist without being neurotic. Again I found in them that inner conflict which is characteristic of modern man: the conflict between a right intuition (namely, that their vocation has fundamental importance for the destiny of humanity) and a false idea (namely, that art is superfluous luxury).

It is not what men produce that unites them, but rather the eternal verities which they can lay hold of only with the heart, generation after generation. A chemist, bred in the dry and barren school of laboratory science, recently related to me a mystical experience he had had. "All of a sudden," he said, "I felt that the man of today lacked something essential, a synthetic sense of that which is above and beyond him." To give back to him this sense, it seems to me, is the task of the new generation, in which it is my hope that philosophers and poets will feel that they are just as useful to humanity as industrialists and scientists.

Today we can observe three kinds of reactions to the repression of the spiritual. And all three of them remind us of the psychology of the adolescent.

I have already mentioned the superstitious reaction. "Chase nature away, and it returns at a gallop." Take away from man the true faith, and he falls victim to the delusion of the illuminati. Thus in our time, which has supposedly rejected all belief which is contrary to reason, there flourishes a superstition that reminds us of the decadence of Rome. And this occurs even in scientific circles. Dr. Paul Dubois[30] jeers at "the scholars, often illustrious" who fall "into the snare of the gross superstitions of spiritualism and telepathy."

Beyond this there is a superstition about science, about medicine, technology, and progress. When the "values" are disavowed, men come to the place where they unconsciously ascribe absolute value to the simple productions of man.

Also a false symbolism flourishes. Men reject the biblical myth of the Fall of man as an outworn naïveté, but they trump up national myths, like Nazism, and even international ones.

The second form of reaction is that of skepticism. Like the adolescent in revolt, modern man hides his inner confusion beneath a skeptical cynicism. By this I mean not merely religious unbelief, but also the bitterness of disillusionment with man himself and with life. "There is no human nature, because there is no God to have a conception of it," writes Sartre.[3] And Nietzsche, reviving Heraclitus' theme of the eternal and fruitless flux of all things, cut out the abiding factor of the Logos which Heraclitus opposed to this perpetual flux. Included here also is the attitude of Gide, with his ideal of detachment and nonengagement. And finally it is that strange god Chance in whom modern scientists blindly believe. "Chance," writes Franck Abauzit,[31] "explains nothing; it is merely the negation of the spirit, the opposite of reason, the destruction of all intelligibility." And yet it is the last word of every scientific explanation of the world. "The classical theory of science," writes Lecomte de Noüy,[32] "simply replaces God with chance. It is nothing more than playing with words." Here again, the psychoanalysts will say, is "the return of the repressed," disguised as in a dream.

Finally, there is the sectarian reaction. Just as the revolting adolescent professes revolutionary doctrines and suffers no contradiction, so modern man throws himself into one contradictory system of thought after another, all of which are marked by the same dogmatism. Dr. René Allendy[5] humorously refers to the preacher who thunders loudly from the pulpit in order to drown out his own haunting doubts. I believe that we find a similar mechanism of compensation at work in our modern world. That is to say, the confusion of minds today is such that many men, in order to reassure themselves, cling with cramped fanaticism to some curious doctrine. In order to still the voice of their inner illness they cast themselves into that sectarian intolerance which involves opposing parties in strife and controversy in all domains of life. When a man is not sure of himself, he pretends to be the man who is unshakably convinced.

Then, too, there is the well-known religious dogmatism. The more living faith grows weaker in the church, the more the church takes refuge in formalism and intolerance. But still the antireligious sectarianism, which characterizes laicism, anticlericalism, the scientific materialism, Nietzsche, or the athestic movement is no less dogmatic. There is the religious sectarianism of all the illuminati who divide the church, the opposition between the different confessional churches, and the sects which claim to be in sole possession of the truth.

In the field of politics, too, we find this sectarian spirit which involves parties and "ideologies" in irreconcilable struggle with one another. And finally, there is a scientific sectarianism. One can arrive at a judgment about it if one observes how sharply the various schools of psychoanalysis feud with one another. And yet, if there is a discipline which ought to impress upon its adepts the relativity of all human doctrines, is it not psychoanalysis?

Tolerance is the natural endowment of true convictions.

Thus modern man, like an adolescent in profound crisis, appears to us to present a strange and contradictory mixture of naïve superstition, disillusioned skepticism, and partisan spirit. For in repressing values, repressing them without having freed himself from them, without ever being able to free himself from them—he has repressed the very principle of his inner harmony: the Spirit.

Chapter II

The Precedence of Personhood

In order to get closer to the problem that concerns us here we shall now examine the way in which the suppression of the spirit reacts upon our conception of the human person. "As an individual the human being belongs to the human species, to society, and consequently to the state . . . but as a person he belongs to God," writes G. de Reynold.[86] Ever since men have suppressed God they have lost the concept of personhood. In the world there are only individuals and states and a perpetual struggle between these two incompatible realities. Alternately liberalism and Communism proclaim the supremacy of the one over the other. But neither liberalism nor Communism give us a concept of man that conforms with nature. Because man has closed his eyes to the world of the Spirit, he has become incomprehensible to himself. He no longer understands himself and he lives in confusion. "The confusion of modern man," writes Dr. Arnold Stocker, "is owing to the fact that he has lost the sense of personhood."[33]

Our scientific civilization, whether it be individualistic or communistic, is an impersonal civilization. Therefore Professor Théophile Spoerri writes, "We must pass through the Renaissance again, but not, as Monnier said, in the sense of the individual, but rather that of the person."[34]

What, then, is the person? What is man?

Everybody knows what direction medical science has pursued for a hundred years now in order to answer that question. It has pursued the direction of materialism. And from that point of view man is compared with a machine, or more precisely, with an assemblage of machines. Just as an automobile is a combination of various machines—cylinders, ignition system, carburetor, headlights, differential, etc.—so man is a complex ensemble of different machines—digestive system, respiratory, nervous, urinary systems, etc.—which, indeed, work together but are nevertheless independent. The ideal of science, then, is to isolate these machines from the assemblage and to study them individually in order to understand how each of them functions. Then each can be reduced to physico-chemical processes which are neither specifically alive nor human.

The synthetic production by chemico-industrial processes of substances which were long believed to be characteristic only of the living organism, such as vitamins and hormones, seemed to be a decisive confirmation of this hypothesis. Thus life is nothing more than the total result of all these inorganic processes. There is, however, one difference between the human machine and the industrial machine with which it is compared, a difference which, paradoxically, makes the human machine even more materialistic than the industrial machine. For in the case of the automobile the combination of the various parts is contrived by an engineer with a view to what the assemblage of the parts will accomplish, whereas in the case of the human being, according to the classic scientific explanation, these different organs and their various chemico-physical functions merely happened by accident to come together to form an organism. Science rejects any argument from design. It is therefore based in particular upon a very disturbing fact: If there are in the organism organs and functions which are indispensable to the whole assemblage, then there are also organs and functions which appear to be of no use.

The liver, for example, is merely a chemical laboratory whose various processes we must take careful note of during the course of our medical studies. Thus science becomes more and more analytical as it distinguishes a constantly increasing number of independent functions in each individual organ. And in pursuing this direction, research has been exceedingly productive of detailed knowledge, but in the process medicine has lost the sense of the person, the sense of man as a whole.

Often this school of thought quite unjustly appeals for authority to Claude Bernard, the brilliant founder of modern physiology. It is true that he opened the way through the experimental study of isolated functions, but, unlike his successors, he never succumbed to the illusion which his labors might suggest. "The vital force," he wrote, "directs the phenomenon which it does not produce; the physical agents produce phenomena which they do not direct." There could be no better expression of the fact that however fruitful the study of chemico-physical processes in the living organism may be, it nevertheless does not pierce the mystery of life. For the mystery of life resides not in the parts but in the whole, in the directing power which is determinative of all the parts. Then, as Claude Bernard goes on to say, "the knowledge of the whole man is the ultimate goal of medicine."

The influence of the moral factor, which is completely ignored by materialistic science, its influence not only upon the emotions and the thinking of the patient but also upon the very substance of his body, likewise did not escape Claude Bernard: "Even a very slight emotional sensation," he wrote, "is sufficient to bring about the temporary appearance of sugar in the urine."

In reality it is not the fault of the French—who have always preserved a certain appreciation of general ideas—nor of the physiologists that medicine eventually took the direction of materialism. It lies rather with German science, with the anatomists, with Virchow,[12] and later with Ehrlich and his attempts to explain by purely chemical means such complex and mysterious biological phenomena as immunity.

I have no wish to deny or to disregard the incomparable contributions of pathological anatomy and physiological chemistry to our knowledge of man. These disciplines, however, have propagated a dogma, namely, that every illness is the result of a lesion. As Dr. Marcel Sendrail[35] points out, this dogma was universally accepted by medical men at the end of the last century. Since in many pathological conditions it was not possible to discover a lesion, they got out of the difficulty by means of a hypothesis. Our present means of investigation, they said, are as yet inadequate to disclose the lesion. This is the so-called organic pathology (*organiciste*), the doctrine of the localization of the disease in an organ. Here we have the comparison of the human body to a machine put forward with all its rigor: just as the mechanic deals with an automobile, so the modern physician confronted by the sick person has one dominant preoccupation: to localize the breakdown.

From this point of view there is no such thing as a general illness but only localized maladies, even if the injury of an organ has a secondary effect upon other organs. Thus, to use Dr. Sendrail's expression, medicine moves in "constant reference to the cadaver."

At the end of the last century the discovery of microbes by Pasteur drove a breach into the "redoubt" of general illness in that it compared the infection caused by a number of local battles or phagocytosis with the poisoning of cells by bacterial toxins. This left the nervous diseases unaccounted for. One may say that at the beginning of this century the physician approached the nervously ill patient, the nonorganically ill, with a certain irritation, which the patient sensed very strongly and which had its basis in the fact that his case could not be fitted into the generally accepted system of medical thought. It was therefore a triumph when the physiologists succeeded in relating Graves' disease [hyperthyroidism], which hitherto had been regarded as a nervous disease, to a lesion of the thyroid gland. From here it was only a step to the expectation that the troublesome area of nervous diseases might gradually be broken down and classified. We remember the tremendous hopes occasioned by the discovery of the brain centers: organic pathology would triumph when it succeeded in determining the organic basis of all psychic and mental functions.

After it had reduced life to chemico-physical phenomena, science was obliged by logic also to seek to reduce thought, consciousness, and spirit to the same thing. And it proceeded to do just this. "The brain as it were digests the impressions," wrote Dr. Cabanis,[36] "and organically produces the secretion of thoughts." Is it necessary today to point out that this is a purely verbal explanation? So strong was the vogue of materialism that the scholar, without perceiving what he was doing, actually departed from the basis of strict scientific observation which he himself had proclaimed to be the only legitimate one. "The materialist conception of epiphenomenal consciousness," writes Dr. Henri Baruk,[13] "according to which consciousness is like a ray of light that emerges from a functioning motor without having any influence whatsoever upon the course of this motor, is so contrary to all the clinical facts that it hardly deserves discussion."

Nevertheless, following physiology, psychology proceeded resolutely to pursue the same path. It set up laboratories in order to study analytically all the functions of the mind and to reduce them to objective processes. We may recall the big noise that was made in our childhood days over the Elberfeld horse. Since it turned out that man could not be entirely compared with a machine, because, after all, he feels and thinks, he was then compared with an animal. By means of experiments upon animals the effort was made to pierce the mystery of intelligence. As Dr. Henri Mentha[25] reports, Dr. Paul Dubois of Berne gave currency to the following joke about materialistic medicine: "The only difference between medicine and the veterinary art is the difference in their clientele."

In a certain respect the work of Freud also falls within this line of development. It is a prolongation of rationalistic materialism, extending it to the whole of psychology, in that it institutes a purely rational analysis of human behavior and attempts to reduce it entirely to animal impulses, the instincts. "Freud," writes Roland Dalbiez,[37] "goes almost to the point of regarding as natural in man only that which he has in common with other animate beings . . . disregarding the human nature of man."

Man, as Freud sees him, is still a machine in that he can be reduced to automatisms and responds to an alleged rigorous psychological determinism. Dalbiez, however, has shown with great clarity that this psychological determinism is something absolutely different from chemico-physical determinism in the sense that the relation between cause and effect which it exhibits can only be demonstrated *a posteriori* and never allows itself to be foreseen.

Nevertheless, viewed from another angle, the work of Freud was actually revolutionary. It broke the line of the development of organic pathological medicine and rediscovered the importance of the psychic. Even before Freud the school of Nancy, by its study of the phenomenon of suggestion, had driven a breach in the dogma of materialism: There are illnesses which are not caused by a lesion but by an idea. At the beginning of the century, Dr. Dubois,[30] the outstanding representative of this school in France, described the great misery of the mentally ill. Innumerable cases, which were unsuccessfully treated according to the medical concepts of that time with drugs, operations, liver and kidney preparations, and hormone therapy, he cured by psychic means. Medicine rediscovered the power of the idea, the reason, the will, the imagination, the emotions. The psychoanalytical school demonstrated the power of the unconscious association of ideas and thus gave considerable breadth to the revolutionary change. Then came the school of Pavlov. As in psychoanalysis one can also distinguish in this school two aspects which seem to be more or less contradictory; on the one hand, it emphasizes the similarity of man to the animal, the possibility of reducing him to machinelike automatisms and, on the other, it demonstrates that the association of ideas governs not only the subjective emotions but also the objective physiological processes.

However that may be, the modern development of medicine confirms the breakdown of the hopes of the last century that it would be able to explain man exclusively by chemico-physical processes. "The life of the mind," writes Dr. Pierre Ponsoye,[38] "cannot be subjected to a yardstick. . . . That is why physiological and psychological phenomena remain incommensurable." And in another place he adds, "The antinomy which exists between the psychic and the physical cannot be eliminated, despite all the efforts to do so."

This has been honestly acknowledged by a representative of the materialistic school such as Jacques Loeb.

But what then?

Why, then if, on the one hand, there are organic diseases caused by lesions and, on the other, nonorganic, functional diseases based on imagination, medicine is split in two. And this is actually the present situation. It is astonishing that in such a rational age as ours medical men should apparently be so little concerned about this. In every clinical case today the physician is confronted with one preliminary question: Is it organic or functional? This is a fundamental demarcation. The whole treatment will be different, depending upon whether the case is assigned to one or to the other of these two categories. We grant that in certain respects the organic pathological view, in which there were no illnesses without a lesion, was more satisfying. The unity of man, the concept of personhood is actually more endangered by our contemporary dualism than it was by the materialistic doctrine.

So here we meet again the great rift between the world of matter and the world of the spirit of which we spoke in the first chapter. And in my opinion it is precisely because modern thinking has accommodated and accustomed itself in its whole view of the world to this opposition between matter and spirit that medical men are so little disturbed by this fundamental dualism. "The error of Descartes," writes Dr. Alexis Carrel,[27] "was to believe in the reality of these abstractions [such as body and soul, matter and spirit] and to consider the material and the mental as heterogeneous, as two different things. This dualism has weighed heavily upon the whole history of our knowledge of man. For it has engendered the false problem of the relations of the soul and the body. There are no such relations. Neither the soul nor the body can be investigated separately. We observe merely a complex being whose activities have been arbitrarily divided into physiological and mental."

Will we be able to find a bridge to carry us over this rift? I believe we shall. I already see the bridgeheads which have been laid on both sides: on the one hand, certain works make it doubtful whether physical processes are conceivable at all if one leaves out the mind, and, on the other, there are certain works which tend to rehabilitate the role of the body in psychic processes.

In the first group is the book by Dr. Jean de Rougemont, professor of surgery at the University of Lyons, *Vie du corps et vie de l'esprit* ["The Life of the Body and the Life of the Spirit"].[11] In this book he shows that the law of life, even in its physical aspects, is the same as the law of the spirit. "Life models the forms, it animates them; it does not construct, it creates. . . ." Farther on he says, "Life makes use of some materials and neglects others. . . . It therefore exercises a choice. . . . In this exact choosing there is evidently a memory and another intelligence at work." So here we have a surgeon, who studies the life of the body, recognizing that all this remains incomprehensible without the concepts of creation, choice, memory, and intelligence, concepts which derive from the world of the spirit.

Now compare with these views what Dr. Arnault Tzanck, chief of medicine in St. Antoine Hospital in Paris, says in his book *La Conscience créatrice* ["The Creative Consciousness"].[23] As Dr. Baruk expresses it, this author "constructs a kind of psychological biology." That is to say, he demonstrates that one cannot explain life without attributing to living matter, the tiniest of our cells, a psychological quality, a memory, and consequently a consciousness from which it originates. "In the last analysis," he writes, "it is the memory which we encounter when we study biological processes." And elsewhere: "Of life one sees nothing but the memory."

In his specialized studies on anaphylaxis, intolerance, and immunity[39] Dr. Tzanck arrives at the same conclusion: "Immunity cannot be explained by materialistic theories, but much more likely by the idea of cell memory. . . . The cells learn to recognize this or that substance and their reaction to it simply follows. . . ." Here, then, we have a surgeon, a laboratory man, a specialist in blood transfusion appealing to psychic ideas in order to explain organic phenomena.

Here again we compare with this quotation what Dr. Georges Menkès says in his book *Médecine sans frontières* ["Medicine without Frontiers"].[40] "Immunity is a phenomenon which affects the nervous system. . . . [it implies] a memory." Dr. Menkès demonstrates with an abundance of evidence that "the nervous system plays an enormous role in pathology, especially in connection with the outbreak of infectious diseases and the development of degenerative diseases." He emphasizes the fact that "basically the deeper laws of infection escape us. . . . How can chilled feet increase the virulence of bacteria which normally inhabit our tonsils?" He quotes Dr. René Allendy who tells the humorous story of how his soldiers during the First World War used to lie on the beds of their comrades who were sick with scarlet fever and yet did not succeed in contracting the illness, as they had hoped, in order to escape being sent to the front. He tells of the amazing experiments of the Russian physician Speransky and his school. By certain irritations of the nerves the Russian scientist succeeded in reproducing organic lesions of exactly the same kind that occur in a local infection. His students went so far as to swallow cultures of cholera bacilli without contracting the disease. Menkès cites the following experiment upon rabbits by Speransky. When he injected toxins while scratching the animal's ear this doctor created a conditioned reflex of such a kind that the rabbits whose ears were not scratched before the fatal dose was injected died, whereas the rest, whose ears had been scratched, survived. Cohn arrived at the same results by frightening guinea pigs. "All this," says Dr. Menkès, "casts doubt upon the real value of classifying diseases organically."

Again a bridge is established between the organic and the functional by Professor Abrami, cited by Dr. Menkès, when he says, "It is the functional disorders that give to the organic diseases their differing faces. Are you not surprised, as I am, at the disproportion that exists between a lesion and its symptoms?" The fact is that this preconceived idea, to which our studies have misled us, namely, that there is a fundamental line of demarcation between organic and functional affections, is not confirmed by clinical observation. All of our patients are both organically and functionally ill. The mind influences the health of the body and produces not only mental troubles but physical disorders which can be observed by clinical examination and in the laboratory. Elsewhere I have given numerous examples of this. Here I have cited Dr. Menkès in order to show that a doctor who by no means adheres to a spiritual view of the world has arrived at the same conclusions purely on the basis of scientific observation. We may also compare this to what Dr. Allendy has written: "One may ask oneself to what extent the maladies which are considered to be purely organic originate from psychic disorders."

As I have said, the bridge between the organic and the functional is being built from both sides of the rift. Indeed, Dr. Philippe Kressmann[41] makes reference to recent studies which seek to demonstrate that there are organic lesions connected with hysteria. On the other hand, Dr. Baruk,[13] whose views I have already stated, gives a purely physiological explanation of psychic and mental disorders. Herein lies a paradox, the significance of which will not escape the physicians among my readers: it goes back to the quarrel between the psychiatrists, who have been called "organicists," and the psychoanalysts. The former clung to organogenesis, the organic provenance of mental disorders, and the latter to the psychogenesis of these disorders. And it appeared that the psychoanalysts, as I have already said, were the pioneers who had rediscovered the importance of the spirit. But what is the spirit or mind of which they, at least the Freudians, speak? Nothing more than animal functions, psychic automatisms. Dr. Baruk has, so to speak, a far more spiritual conception of the spirit. For him it means the moral consciousness, the conscience, the perception of good and evil, the sense of justice and humanity. Without denying the processes studied by the psychoanalysts, especially that of the incomplete repression of instinct, Dr. Baruk goes on to say, "The question that remains to be clarified is that of the cause of these mischievous repressions; . . . their mechanisms are far more complex" than Freud thought they were when he spoke merely of "social inhibition." Our author then says of these complex factors: "In the first place there are causes of a physiological kind, toxic processes, vascular influences. . . ." We note that Dr. Baruk is at the same time more of a spiritualist and more of an organicist than the psychoanalysts. "One must study without bias," writes Dr. Roger Reyss,[14] "without forgetting that man, even the mentally ill man, is body and soul; to neglect the one is to disembody or to animalize the other. . . ."

So today in medicine the great rift between matter and spirit, the organic and the functional is not far from being filled. In the book to which we have already referred,[2] Dr. Alphonse Maeder speaks of a case of "hyperthyroidlike illness." He calls it "hyperthyroidlike" since the physician who referred the case to him had noted "the eye condition typical of Graves' disease —exophthalmus, infrequent eyelid movement, rigidity and weakness of the adductor muscles of the eye ball" and tachycardia though the metabolic rate was only increased by 12.5%. In reality, I believe that in Italian Switzerland such a case would be called *"Basedow fruste"* [pseudo-hyperthyroid], since we have, more than our confederates, preserved the French tradition of the primacy of the clinic over the laboratory. In any case Dr. Maeder himself raises the problem: "One may ask oneself whether such a case should be viewed as a *forme fruste* or as an early stage of hyperthyroid." He then goes on to say: "If, indeed, the psychotherapeutic intervention herein described is able to influence the autonomic-vegetative nervous system so rapidly and effectively, as demonstrated here after the second visit, then, conversely, the stiffening and undue increase of the psychic and physical need could have favored the transformation to the organic of the originally psychoneurotic and actual neurotic process (thyroid disease, increase in the metabolic rate, etc.)."

Do we not have here an idea that is very fruitful and very satisfactory? Are not many illnesses at the beginning functional and then later become organic? Does not the body in time allow to develop into a lesion what at first was only a functional disorder? When I am sad and go about with a bent back I can straighten up again whenever I wish to do so. But if I remain in a stooped position for years, my spinal column is eventually modified; it will organically fixate my bad posture, which at the beginning was purely a mental attitude. Does not the same apply to the wrinkles in our hands, the lineaments of our faces, the amplitude of our respiration and undoubtedly the metabolism of the liver or of our red blood corpuscles? At the beginning there are functional disorders for which neither clinical examination of the organs nor the laboratory can discover any physical sign; later a lesion has formed which can be observed and measured.

The closing of the rift between the organic and the functional will mean a step toward a new conception of man.

Yes, we need to recover a satisfactory conception of man. The physician possesses precise knowledge of the metabolism of calcium, the digestion of fats, and the mechanism of dreams; but of the human person as a whole he has no idea. After the era of materialism in which man was compared with a machine, after the psychoanalytical episode which added psychological

mechanisms to the physico-chemical mechanisms and compared
man with the animal, after allowing a rift to exist between matter and spirit, medicine has a nostalgia for a synthesis. Dr. Roger
Reyss[14] recounts the case of "a twenty-two-year-old employee who
was suddenly seized with an incoherent persecution mania, was
no longer able to sleep, constantly believed that someone was
going to kill him, saw men clothed in black coming to shoot
him, and threw himself out of a window in order to escape
them. . . . After an acute seizure of diarrhea he returned to
normal in two days, retaining only a hazy memory of what had
happened. . . . He had already had numerous attacks of urticaria, a curious and transitory history of pulmonary trouble, a
tenacious, painful attack of colitis, and for a long time had been
treated without success for intestinal worms." And the physician
makes this significant comment: "Perhaps all this hangs together.
Perhaps his mental illness, as well as the urticaria, for example,
was only an episode in the history of his illness."

Yes, our spirit will be truly satisfied only if medicine finally
enables us to understand why it is that one and the same illness
expresses itself sometimes in physical phenomena and sometimes in psychic or mental phenomena. After all, what physician
has not observed that in numerous cases a physical improvement
is accompanied by a psychic aggravation or, conversely, that the
illness manifests itself alternately in one manner or in the other?
In order better to understand the sick person there can be no
doubt that one should first of all, to use the words of Dr. Mentha,[25]
"renounce all premature diagnosis, all definitive classification in
water-tight categories," to which the analytical tendency of contemporary medicine may easily lead us. Modern medicine must
rediscover the influence of the body upon the mind and the
influence of the mind upon the body, something of which the
ancients were not unaware. A hundred years ago Trousseau
cited the case of an asthmatic who had become so sensitive to
violets that she suffered an attack at the sight of a bouquet of
artificial violets. Therefore, there must be a unity of the person.

"The body," writes Dr. Ponsoye,[38] "can receive from the soul health, sickness, or death. . . . Death through syncope (fainting) is sufficient to give us an idea of the dynamic potency of cerebral cortex." And Dr. Jean de Rougemont[11] writes: "One must accept that one and the same power provides the secretions of our glands and animates our most sublime thoughts."

Now, is this power nothing else but that psyche* of the physiologists and the psychoanalysts, which is to say, an assemblage of nervous functions, animal urges? The importance of the nervous functions, which are studied by psychology, is no longer denied. "A sharp separation between the body and the psyche is not possible," writes Dr. Agostino Maltarello.[42] "All doctors now admit this; the denial of the psyche is a part of a materialism which has been definitely superseded. But this is not to say that all medical men accept the Christian conception of life, that they believe in the immortality of the soul and the supernatural destiny of man."

Therefore, even though all medical men today recognize the existence of the psyche, they are not yet agreed as to the meaning of the term "soul." Or rather, a number of them believe that besides the "soul" in the psychological sense of the word there is in man a soul in the spiritual sense of the word. Was not man, as the Bible says, the object of a special creation of God, who bestowed upon him a specific character which distinguishes him from the animals? What, then, is the human "person": a body, psychological functions, or something else and something more?

Many authors are seeking to answer that question today. This "something else and something more" is, for Dr. Ponsoye,[38] love in the metaphysical sense of the term, for Dr. Stocker,[33] the heart in Pascal's sense of the word, for Dr. de Rougemont[11]

---

* Here and in what follows the word *âme* is normally translated as "psyche," but this cannot be done consistently since the context frequently demands the word "soul." *Esprit* is normally translated "spirit." Dr. Tournier's own discussion reveals the confusion in the use of these terms. (Trans.)

as well as for myself, the spirit. Now, whether one designates this "something" by the term love, heart, or spirit, one obviously intends to convey that it is a reality which cannot be apprehended by science, a reality which has been "repressed" by the modern world, one of those realities which it has reduced to the rank of a negligible hypothesis, which in our study of the world and of man we can leave out of account. It is a religious reality: "Religion," writes Dr. de Rougemont, "is the recognition of the supreme power of life."[11]

Thus, according to many authors, a complete conception of the "person" can be recovered only if we resolutely abandon our habit of opposing to each other the world of the spirit, religion, philosophy, poetry, and the world of the body, the material, economics.

Therefore attempts have been made to formulate a kind of scheme or diagram of the whole person. The following scheme has been proposed by Dr. Jean de Rougemont in his book *Vie du corps et vie de l'esprit.*[11]

Human life, he says, manifests itself through:

1. bodily, physical phenomena (everybody knows what is meant by this);

2. psychic phenomena: the play of imagination, mental images, the interior sense;

3. mental phenomena: abstract thinking, judgment, reasoning, willing;

4. unconscious phenomena;

5. spiritual phenomena: ideal, reasonableness (fairness), love.

Strictly speaking the unconscious phenomena do not constitute a particular "storey"; rather the phenomena of the second and the third storeys (perhaps, according to Dr. Baruk, also the fifth storey) may be conscious or unconscious. The scheme therefore includes only four storeys: physical life, psychic life, mental life, spiritual life.

The distinction between storeys two and three seems to me to be proper, since the mental and intellectual is peculiar to man, whereas he has the psychic in common with the animal. On the other hand, the mental phenomena are clearly different from the spiritual phenomena.

Dr. de Rougement lays particular emphasis upon the indissoluble unity of the whole. "We are 'men' through our body, our psyche, our mind, our unconscious, and our spirit. . . . there are no sharp boundaries."

Now let us compare this scheme with that which Dr. Stocker gives us in his book *Désarroi de l'homme moderne* ["The Confusion of Modern Man"].[33] It constitutes a cone, the point of which (*a*) represents the heart in the Pascalian sense (which Dr. de Rougemont and I call the spirit). The middle part (*b*) represents the spirit (by which Dr. Stocker means the intellect, and therefore chiefly the "mental" in de Rougemont's sense of the term). The base (*c*) represents the body.

As we see, the two schemes can be superimposed upon each other:

1 for de Rougemont = *c* for Stocker
2, 3 for de Rougemont = *b* for Stocker
5 for de Rougemont = *a* for Stocker

As Dr. Stocker goes on to say, there are three modes of gaining knowledge: through the body, through the spirit (intellect), and through the heart (love).

Using the literary method which is his habit, Dr. Stocker illustrates his scheme by examples borrowed from Paul Valéry and André Gide. In *Dans la Soirée avec M. Teste* ["Evening with Mr. Teste"], *Lettre d'un ami* ["Letter from a Friend"], and *Lettre de Mme. Emilie Teste* ["Letter from Madame Emilie Teste"], Valéry symbolizes the heart (*a*) by Madame Teste, the spirit (*b*) by Mr. Teste, and the body (*c*) by the friend. In *La Porte étroite* [*Strait is the Gate*] by Gide, Alissa represents the heart (*a*), Jerome the spirit (*b*), and Juliette the body (*c*).

What was it that inspired Dr. Stocker to adopt this cone-shaped structure? It was doubtless the expression "the fine point of the soul" by which Francis de Sales describes that "something" which makes man a spiritual being, distinct from the animal, and which Stocker calls "heart" and de Rougemont calls "spirit." For this "fine point" is the point of the cone. A Catholic physician like Dr. Stocker is of course bound by Thomist philosophy and its "hylomorphism," that is, the affirmation of Thomas Aquinas that man is composed only of two constituents, body and soul, the soul being, according to the Aristotelian view, the "form of the body."

Consequently, the Catholic doctor cannot assign to the spirit a special "storey." Nevertheless he knows that the psychological soul of the physiologists and psychoanalysts dare not be confounded with the spiritual soul which is peculiar to man. He therefore describes this latter by the expression "fine point of the soul."

However that may be, we see that Dr. Stocker, despite Thomistic doctrine, distinguishes between spirit and soul, or, to use his terminology, between heart and spirit, which he designates by the two letters a and b. This is what made it possible for us to superimpose the two schemes in order to show that in reality the Catholic and the Protestant doctor arrive at the same view of man.

One can, I think, raise an objection to these two schemes. The arrangement into "storeys" may suggest the idea that the spiritual element which is peculiar to man is just one more storey like the others, comparable to the others and simply a truncated cone added to the top of the animal part of man (1, 2, 3 in de Rougemont's scheme or b and c in Stocker's).

Yet everyone perceives that the nature of the spirit is different. The lower storeys are accessible to science, to objective examination. One can make body, psyche, and the mind the object of experiment. The spirit, however, is inaccessible to science; it can be perceived only intuitively, introspectively, or better, though grace.

Moreover, this division into "storeys" may also suggest that the spirit borders upon the mental or the psychic but not upon the physical, that it does not govern the body except through the intermediation of the soul. This idea strikes me as being contrary to the Christian view of man, with the concept of the incarnation. Dr. Kütemeyer of Heidelberg University, in a conference on the relation of modern medicine to the doctrines of the church at the Evangelical Academy, Bad Boll, said something that seemed to me to be of great importance to the discussion of our view of man. "For the Christian," he said, "the spirit is not farther away from the body than is the soul." In consequence of the intellectualistic degeneration of our civilization, which affected the church as well as the world, in consequence of the fact that one can express spiritual things only by means of words and abstract ideas, in short, by means of "mental phenomena," and finally in consequence of the old Platonic opposition between perishable matter and immortal soul, which is still so deeply rooted in modern philosophy as well as in the Christian church, we may fall into the dangerous belief that the soul is more spiritual than the body.

In reality the spirit, the "breath of life" which God breathed into the nostrils of man, became incarnate in the whole of the human animal, in his body as well as in his psyche or his mind; it animates all of them, it expresses itself in each one of them. If, for example, we regard love as being one of the essential attributes of the spirit—as de Rougemont, Stocker, and Ponsoye all do—then it is clear that we can express this love through a look or a clasp of the hand (that is, the body) just as well as through our imagination (psyche) or an abstract idea (mind). These considerations lead me to propose a third scheme:

It can be represented by an equilateral triangle. In the triangle the three bisectors delimit three small triangles which represent the body (A), the psyche (B), and the mind (C). The spirit is here represented only by a nonspatial "geometrical point," the point at which the bisectors intersect, the center. It is the center of the person, around which the whole man is ordered. It is invisible, it has no dimensions, and is not directly accessible. From the outside it is perceptible only through one of the three constituents A, B, C. Moreover it manifests itself outwardly and perceives exterior reality only through one of these three functions: its body, its imagination, or its thinking.

Thus the spirit would be the essence of the human person. The philosophers will quarrel with me over this term, which they consider to be their private property. But what does it matter? The spirit dwells in the heart of the person: we thus come back to the term which Stocker used and its "fine point," a purely geometrical point, except that it is not only the fine point of the soul, but always the common point of the body, the psyche, and the mind.

Thus the spirit expresses itself through the body, A; that is to say, through gestures and through material and economic things. It expresses itself through the psyche, B; that is, through imagination, through feelings, through art. And it expresses itself finally through the intellect, through the mind, through ideas, C; that is, through theology.

Since our civilization has founded knowledge solely upon objective exterior investigation, it is condemned to a comprehension of man which is limited to his exterior: A, B, and C— and to remain ignorant of his spiritual essence, the spirit which is inaccessible from the outside. But the spirit is what gives meaning to the body, the psyche, and the mind and at the same time assures their harmony, their articulation, their unity. Each of the three elements, A, B, and C, touches the other two and influences them: the body influences the psyche and the mind; the mind influences the psyche and the body; and the psyche influences the body and the mind. But the spirit in the center determines their limits and their harmony. The spirit constitutes the center of polarization of the person.

Dr. Joseph Zwiebel[43] tells us that before his conversion to Christianity he based his entire ethics upon the idea of human equality. Afterward he no longer regarded man as his "like," but rather as his "neighbor." This means that suddenly he discovered what gives to every man his specifically human character: the spirit, which is his essence and the source of a new bond between men, the love of one's neighbor, which is far more profound than the feeling of their likeness. "Men are different," he writes, "but they are neighbors. Men are persons in whom God's spirit has become incarnate."

Therefore, in order to recover the meaning of personhood and its unity, we must learn again that it is the spirit which we perceive through the manifestations of its physical, psychic, and mental envelope. Ultimately it is the spiritual destiny of man which is being played out in his physical and economic destiny, in his psychological and artistic destiny, and in his mental and intellectual destiny.

A new and very important concept evolves from these three schematic representations which I have set before the reader, namely, the concept of a hierarchy of the human forces or constituents. Whether one takes the successive "storeys" of de Rougemont's scheme, Stocker's cone, or my triangle, one will always have an unfailing order in this whole, always a clear framework.

Of the "five ways of manifestation" which he enumerates, writes Dr. de Rougemont, "only two are conformed to the fulfilment of the law of life. . . . the body and the spirit." One finds, therefore, in de Rougemont a vindication of the body. And he goes on to say: "I cannot subscribe to the common opinion which sees in the flesh an obstacle to the flowering of the spirit and regards it with great distrust or utter contempt. . . . And yet our intelligence, our sensibility, our judgment, our will (in other words, the intermediate "storeys") can make use of our muscles and organs in order to cause them to perform acts which are detrimental to physiological equilibrium and at the same time contrary to the spirit." "If the life of man is troubled despite the natural docility of the body and the spirit, this is

possible only through the interposition of conscious or unconscious psychic and mental elements and above all through the
abnormal development of the psyche and the mind."

We see, then, that there we have a fundamental hypothesis
to explain "the drama of the self"; the fault is assigned to the
intermediate storey, the psychic and mental element.

Actually, the needs of the body are justified and extinguished
as soon as they are satisfied. It is the imagination and the intellect, asserting their freedom from the normal, healthy laws
of life, that conceive the "desire," the thirst for hypertrophic,
unlimited, insatiable gratification, sentimental or intellectual.
Original sin is not, as is commonly believed, so much a fleshly
sin as a psycho-mental sin, as symbol of the "tree of knowledge"
indicates. It is the craving for knowledge and gratification beyond those limits that are set by his physical and spiritual needs
which has precipitated man into his misfortune. This is due, in
the last analysis, to a psycho-mental autonomy asserting its freedom from the hierarchical authority of the spirit. The reader
may compare with these considerations what we have said concerning the crisis of man since the Renaissance. As a matter of
fact the movement to free the intellect and the imagination from
the bounds of the spiritual has assumed gigantic proportions
since the Renaissance. The autonomy of reason, of thought, and
imagination has been proclaimed. And it is not difficult for Dr.
de Rougemont to show that this hypertrophy of the intellectual
and the psychic is the profound source of the convulsions of
the modern world. The desire, the thirst for pleasure is plunging
man into misfortune; for man is "achieving a paradoxical result:
he is spoiling the very instrument of his pleasure."

The hierarchy of the person: there is a healthy and proper
hierarchy in which the body, the psyche, and the mind are
subordinated to the spirit. When this order of precedence is
disturbed there is no longer any harmony. Dr. de Rougemont
has given us a good simile for this: a telescope whose lenses
have been reversed.

THE PRECEDENCE OF PERSONHOOD 57

"Man," wrote Dr. Georges Liengme,[44] "is a complex being. He has within him a vegetative, an animal, and a human life, which must be coordinated and unified by being penetrated by a higher, spiritual life." And Leslie Weatherhead[45] writes: "God alone . . . can . . . allow the personality to become a harmonious unity."

We find this same concept of the hierarchy of the person in what Dr. Stocker has written. Recall his figure of a cone and its order, *a, b, c*. Only this order, *a b c*, is healthy and assures the equilibrium of the person; it stands securely on its base and is governed by its summit. There are five other possible combinations. The first four (*a c b, b a c, b c a, c a b*) are those of the "sick person," the "neurotic." And one understands, then, why there are so many disordered people in the world. These types correspond, one understands, to the hypertrophy of the intermediate storeys in de Rougemont's scheme. Finally, the last possible combination, *c b a*, preserves the right order of the components, but in reverse sequence. This, says Stocker, is the "perverted person." Instead of a stable cone, we have a "spinning top" with its supremacy of the body over the mind and the mind over the heart. "Of all the deformations the 'perverted' is also the most 'dynamic'; but this spinning top cannot hold itself 'upright' unless it keeps turning, driven, you must understand, by the lash of the senses, the sensuality which, in this case, has supplanted the heart."[33]

The reader will readily compare Stocker's "perverted" person with Baruk's "*folies lucides*," which I mentioned above, those most dangerous of all beings in whom the eclipse of the spirit is in such sharp contrast with the integrity of their physical, mental, and psychic functions.

Thus in medicine there is developing an entirely new and, in my opinion, extremely fruitful idea. True, there are illnesses which are due to a local disturbance, to a change in an organ or to a definite psychological repression. Illnesses of this kind were the only ones that were conceivable when man was envisaged as a machine. In such cases the old slogan retains its value: localize the disturbance in order to remedy it. But there are other illnesses, organic as well as functional, which result essentially, not from an alteration of a part of the machine, but rather from a disharmony of the whole person and may even allow each individual part of the machinery to remain intact. For health does not depend solely upon the integrity of the various parts, but rather upon the proper hierarchy of the whole. This is what I called positive health in my book *Médecine de la personne*.

On this subject Dr. Stocker has given us a good metaphor: that of a factory and its director. For the normal functioning of the factory it is not enough that each department be well organized; the individual departments as a whole must be subject to the authority of the director. The work of the director remains, as it were, invisible to those who visit the factory; they see only the mass of machines. One can only sense the role which the director plays in the co-ordination of the whole enterprise. If each department seeks to be independent, even assuming that it is functioning well and is seeking independence in order to accomplish more work, the factory is disorganized. In this metaphor we find once more the excessive irruption of the imagination and the intellect which, as Dr. de Rougemont says, has upset the modern world. The various departments achieve an orderly, harmonious co-operation with one another only as each performs exactly the particular function which has been assigned to it by the director.

In his study of consciousness, Dr. Baruk falls back upon the same metaphor. It will be recalled that for him consciousness means not only the consciousness of the self, but moral consciousness (the conscience), concepts which the German (and the English) language distinguishes by means of two different words, whereas the French language has, not without reason, reunited them. Consciousness as moral consciousness, as judgment concerning good and evil is thus for Dr. Baruk not a psychological or mental reality, but rather a spiritual reality. It is the peculiar element of that which he calls the "deeper personality" and we call the "spirit." He writes, "Consciousness does not represent a simple apparatus to gain information. It represents the directing and animating thinking; without it our psychological life would be no more than a machine without a director, a factory without a manager, a mass of forces without a guide."[13]

Finally, Dr. Stocker draws from his metaphor still another conclusion. A good director should direct and should not himself work in the shop or interfere in the inner organization of each department. Under his authority his departmental heads must enjoy a certain individual initiative. In this way they relieve him of a thousand secondary concerns, in order that he, the director, may devote himself to his proper task.

The same thing is true of the automatic functions of our physical and psychological life, each of our organs and our psychomental mechanisms. These automatisms disburden the spirit in that they all subordinate themselves to the orders of the whole person. Here we encounter again the thoughts of Dr. Tzanck.[23] He remarks that in biology everything appears to proceed automatically and yet everything appears to be contributing to one chosen goal of a creative consciousness. This consciousness always remains invisible to objective exploration, but nevertheless is indispensable to the comprehension of life.

We now leave the area of metaphor and theoretical schemes of the person in order to come back to a discussion of how the human organism actually functions. For everything we have said concerning the precedence of the person and the supremacy of the spirit has a very definite and practical meaning. This I would now like to demonstrate, and in doing so I follow Dr. Pierre Ponsoye in his book *L'Esprit, force biologique fondamentale* ["The Spirit, Fundamental Biological Force"].[38]

"In the sea urchin," he writes, "the nervous activity appears to be like a 'republic of reflexes,' but as soon as the symmetry of the nerve centers becomes apparent, the coordination and hierarchical subordination, which reaches its pinnacle in the human brain, becomes apparent." This co-ordination of all the functions of the body through the nervous system is well known. The nervous system not only ensures the functions of relation, of sensation and movement, but also governs the processes of growth and the chemical processes of the organism through the medium of the internal secretions which it regulates. Well known also is the respective dependence of the various nerve centers, the spinal cord upon the medulla oblongata, the medulla oblongata upon the central gray matter, and this in turn upon the cerebral cortex. Dr. Ponsoye mentions these facts in order to develop from them an evident truth based upon observation, namely, that the farther up one goes on the animal scale the more do the originally autonomous lower centers become dependent upon the higher centers and thereafter are unable to function normally without their influence. Thus a dog whose brain has been removed continues to live a vegetative life, which is governed by its lower centers, whereas a man deprived of his cerebral cortex dies, despite the integrity of his vegetative centers, since these are no longer capable, as in the dog, of functioning without the control of the brain, the seat of the spirit.

The activity of the lower centers, adds Dr. Ponsoye—and this recalls the metaphor of the director of a factory—has "the primary consequence of freeing the brain from concern for the body, all the while subjecting it to itself as the specific instrument of its operation."

Here we touch upon the problems of the nervosity of modern man, the growing tide of nervously ill people so familiar in our time. "The emotional manifestations," writes Dr. Ponsoye, "represent an archaic type of phenomenon, which in our time should actually be mastered by the cerebral cortex and . . . their appearance always indicates a temporary state, slight or grave, or cortical insufficiency and a disturbance in the patient's general attitude toward the world."

The reader will grasp the importance of this observation. In man, contrary to the animal, the lower centers are so constituted that they function normally only when they are subjected to the authority of the spirit through the medium of the cerebral cortex. If the spirit is repressed, if the "central inhibition" which it should exercise is suspended, if that dismissal of the spirit, which is so general in our modern world, occurs, then the vegetative functions, like the department heads in a factory, assume a relative autonomy, and this results in disordered emotional reactions and functional disturbances. Here we have laid our finger upon the practical significance of the hierarchy of the person. We understand why the vegetative neurosis is so widespread today. It is the result of the fact that the spirit has lost the precedence which it is meant to have.

Finally, Dr. Ponsoye, after having recalled the successive steps in the development of the nerve centers in the animal scale, emphasizes the importance of the most recent part of the brain, the neocerebellum, which in man has developed to a degree unknown in the animal and which "preserves an impressionability which the organism no longer possesses." The cerebral localizations, that is to say, the centers of command for the various vegetative functions as well as sensation and movement constitute only a small part of the human brain. It remains "an enormous mass of non-specific tissue." It was not long ago that doctors educated only in the school of positive science were still saying: "The greater part of the brain serves no purpose at all." But there is no doubt whatsoever that here is the seat of the ever moving tide of conditioned reflexes which give to our psychic and mental life, even in its highest spheres, its peculiarly human physiognomy. The destruction of the neocerebellum results in "the loss of the others" and the exaltation of the automatisms and instincts. The organism, thrown back upon its own resources, becomes indifferent to the world, and deprived of the spiritual faculty which is love, then functions like a machine.

But the fact is that all these nerve centers, the most automatic as well as the most submissive to control, the neocerebellum, have been placed under the regulative authority of the cerebral cortex, the seat of consciousness. "What goes on," writes Dr. Ponsoye, "in this thin and fragile outer layer where, for some, matter engenders spirit but, for others, spirit becomes matter? . . . The spirit guards the secret of its essential character. It also guards the secret of how it flows into matter, from which, in accord with its essential nature, it affirms its independence. It remains for us a datum, whose source and cause we do not know, and the most singular form of energy to be found in life."

What is it, our author asks himself again, that thus impels the spirit to become incarnate? "It is the instinct of life . . . which has a name in human language: it is love."

Here we have returned, then, by the detour of scientific study, to the metaphysical problem of the person. "The biological problem of man," writes Dr. Ponsoye, "is . . . a metaphysical problem." Later on he states this more precisely: "The solution of the biological problem of man presupposes a deliberate return to metaphysic understanding and a commitment without reserve of the person who cares (the physician) to the person who suffers (the patient)."

Dr. Viktor von Weizsäcker[16] has given the right counsel for contemporary medicine: "Treat the whole person"; and then goes on to say: "This tremendous and monstrous pretension on the part of the physician, though it is imposed upon him by the need of his patient, is justified only if his procedure and his therapeutic action is based upon an ontological concept of man."

In order, therefore, to recover the sense of personhood, we shall have to put an end to the repression of the spirit, philosophy, and poetry, which we described in the first chapter. We shall have to resolve to study man, not merely from the outside, through scientific investigation, but also from the inside, through intuitive knowledge, through the spiritual communion which establishes a person-to-person bond between the physician and his patient.

I hardly need say that today all physicians are not yet convinced of this. Many wish to remain faithful to the scientific prejudice which excludes from medicine any spiritual, philosophical, or religious interference whatsoever. But medicine is arbitrarily and regrettably limiting its horizon when it refrains from entering upon the moral domain. Where is the boundary between the physical and the spiritual suffering of humanity? "Man suffers," writes Dr. Agostino Maltarello,[42] "and the causes of his suffering do not lie solely in illnesses of his body. There are pains of a moral order which far surpass those that are physical. On the other hand there are physical ills that have their roots in moral disorders, in the passions, in excessive attachment to personal desires, in insensate love of self and one's fellow creatures, in feelings of hatred, meanness, egotism, and cupidity."

Moreover, an attentive observer will perceive in this common origin of physical and spiritual illnesses a fundamental human distress, a metaphysical anxiety. Henri Ochsenbein, in his fine book *Les compagnons de la vie* ("The Companions of Life"),[46] uses the happy expression "the sickness of life" to characterize this ill and compares it with homesickness. All men, he says, seek life: "In vain we try all the variations in order to get it. We change uniforms, masks, façades, environments, habits; some people change their women, others their religion, their church; nations change their governments and institutions . . . and always there remains the mysterious sickness that stubbornly accompanies us through all the changes: the sickness of life."

Of course it is very difficult to define the domain of this illness, precisely because it goes beyond all our human categories. As Dr. Mentha so rightly says, it is "a vague area, a kind of no-man's-land, of which one does not know whether it belongs.

to medicine, to psychology, or to religion." And in our present society the patient who is ill with "the sickness of life" finds it hard to discover the well-rounded doctor he needs.

Nevertheless, one can see in the medical profession a growing concern for the human person. "In the last twenty years among men of science as well as general practitioners," writes Dr. Kressman of Bordeaux,[41] "among the agnostics as well as believers, there has become evident the need for a more human science, a view of medicine that is able to see the human being as he is and not as one imagines him to be or deduces him to be from experiments made upon animals or from too hastily generalized laws." "Where medicine was prone to see a 'standard mechanism' consisting of interchangeable parts," he continues, "it has now discovered an indivisible whole in which every part is a function of its neighboring part and with them constitutes an ensemble that evidences its own peculiar marks of character: a person." Today, with the tendency of medicine toward specialization, it happens that the sick person is treated by numerous doctors for every one of his organs and yet cannot entrust his "person" to anyone. "Medicine," says Dr. Mentha,[25] "must accept the idea which is current in other areas, the concept of the *foreman*. One of the physicians implicated in the treatment must assume this office—possibly the psychologist or even the minister. For the sick person should not be divided among several influences, nor dare he be left to himself in loneliness and not knowing to whom he should turn." "The characteristic mark of the medicine of the person," Dr. Mentha writes, "is the fact that it keeps its eye on the sick person with his body, with his mind, and with his spirit and not upon this or that practice, this system or that instrument. This medicine goes beyond physical medicine, without our being able to assign exact limits to it and without being able to foresee whom the physician may draw into collaboration in a given case."

Although the necessary medical specialization must continue to exist and indeed be further advanced, one sees, even among the specialists, a wholly new sense of responsibility for the whole person.

In the United States the term "psychosomatic medicine" has met with success, because it manifestly corresponds to the clinical observation of a great number of cases. In an illness, writes de Rougemont, "the organism and the psycho-mental are always simultaneously affected." I remind you that this physician is a surgeon. This general movement of contemporary medicine toward a search for a medicine of the person, which I describe here, is by no means a movement of psychiatrists only. It is concerned with much more than neuroses or functional disorders. It has in view the illness, the whole illness, the whole person. It is specifically concerned to fill the gap which had been opened up between the domain of the body and the domain of the spirit.

Here I must mention the numerous works of Dr. Pierre Delore[47] of Lyons, an internist and hygienist, in which he develops the concept of incarnation and of a "psycho-physiology," that is to say, a physiology which is properly human, distinct from the physiology which is common to both man and animal. Another surgeon, Professor Gosset of Paris, recently presented to the Society for Surgery a paper on "Surgery and Psychosomatic Medicine."

Instead of a quarrel between the psychoanalysts, who refused to contemplate anything but "psychogenesis," and the organicists, who saw only physico-chemical causes, we are now witnessing a movement toward a synthesis which is returning to the views of Christianity, the religion of the incarnation. "The spirit lives to the extent that it incarnates itself," writes Dr. Ponsoye. But he goes on to say, ". . . it dies to the extent that it allows itself to be dominated by the instrument of its incarnation." We quote once more the theologian Robert Schütz,[48] who writes: "By 'person' we mean man in all his humanity, body, mind and spirit."

For my own part I believe that the psychosomatic movement

is an important step on the way toward the discovery of the person. But only a step. The mind in the psychological sense of the word, the sense intended by the physiologists and the psychoanalysts still consists, to use Dr. Odier's[49] term, only in "functions." This doctor recognizes, in contrast with Freud, that there are true "values," that is, spiritual values, beyond these "functions." The "functions" constitute at most an individual. It is the "values" that constitute a person.

The spirit, the divine in man, utilizes these physiological and psychological functions in order to express itself. For it is the spirit which is the secret of the mysterious articulation of these functions. This view alone gives us a synthetic, a whole, view of man. It alone gives back to medicine the human character it has so largely lost. "Medicine," writes Dr. Mentha,[25] "will be humanized and vivified in the same measure as doctors rediscover the sources of revealed truth, which is not, like scientific truth, subject to the conditions of time, space, and number."

There may be local disorders in the physiological and psychological functions. A specialized therapy may well be able to restore order for a time. But this is only a local, not a general cure, a superficial, not a profound cure. These local and occasional disorders are sporadic accidents of a more general malady, and this has its basis in the spiritual destiny of the man involved.

Illnesses are in a sense symbolic. They can be regarded scientifically as determined accidents, the mechanism of which is investigated by science. But all of them can also be regarded symbolically as accidents which were bound to happen, as elements in the destiny of man, as symbols of this general illness of man from which he has suffered unceasingly, and has done so ever since that first day when he shattered the harmonious and healthy nature that God had given to him. Even death is not merely a physiological and psychological phenomenon; it is the great event in the spiritual destiny of man.

"Faith in a Providence that governs the world with infinite wisdom," writes Dr. Maltarello,[42] "certainly does not permit us to plumb the ultimate depths of the mystery of suffering. It does, however, give us a key to its partial solution. That is to say, it sees in sin the deepest cause of the evils that afflict mankind, in such a way that all pathology can thus be connected with the disobedience of the first man." And Dr. Maltarello goes on to say: "The Christian doctor . . . is inspired with a deep humility. He knows that if God permits evil, he does so in order that something good of inestimable value may come out of it. He knows that the salvation of the soul is infinitely more precious than the healing of the body. God can choose various ways to touch souls. The way of suffering, physical as well as mental, appears to be the most natural and is also the most frequent. Pain brings us close to Christ, to him who ransomed mankind by offering himself a victim for it. The sick person is our brother in whom through all the centuries Christ completes his passion and fulfills his work of saving souls."

Science and technology enable us to treat the "local disorders." This does not demand of us the commitment of our own person; we can remain quite objective in the process. But the sickness of man, the break that occurred in his spiritual destiny, we can get at only as we ourselves are healed of it. "The image of the doctor of the future," writes Dr. Ponsoye, "is that of a light-bringer, a man who is himself purified in order to be able to purify others, who takes upon himself the burden of human pain in order to know and to heal it."[38]

CHAPTER III

The Rift between
the Spiritual and the Temporal

IN OUR FIRST chapter, we attempted to set down a diagnosis of the sickness of our broken modern world. We compared this world with an anxiety-ridden adolescent who appears to be in conflict with his parents, his teachers, and society, but who is in reality in conflict with himself, that is, with his better self, which is his repressed moral consciousness.

In the second chapter, we showed by reference to the works of various contemporary doctors that we have forgotten something in our study of man during the course of these last centuries; that we have closed our eyes to that which is specifically human in man, that which some call the spirit, others the heart, still others love or moral consciousness; that the human personality becomes incomprehensible in its unity if one ignores the hierarchical principle, the law of precedence; and finally, that herein lies the reason for the strange powerlessness of medicine—which is so skillful in repairing local lesions—in the face of the rising flood of maladies connected with the inner disharmony of man.

Now I must show how these two orders of facts, those of the modern world and those of modern man, are interrelated and why we are justified in arguing from the illnesses of the person to the illnesses of the world.

And here again it is Dr. Henri Baruk,[13] chief of medicine

at the Maison nationale de Charenton, who helps us through his studies of hate feelings. Everyone will understand the importance of such studies, since one of the essential symptoms of the sickness of the modern world is eruptions of hate without parallel in history which defy all the efforts of statesmen who are responsible for the health of the world. If medical science in some new way succeeds in throwing unexpected light upon the unconscious origin of hate feelings, it will really have something important to say to our contemporary world, to statesmen, economists, and the leaders of culture and public life.

We have seen that Dr. Baruk describes in man a "deeper personality," which is distinct from his physiological, psychological, and mental functions. Science is not adequate to recognize it; in order to do so a communion of heart must be established. The doctor needs "a whole new art . . . in order to discover this deeper personality which is hidden and unexpressed, in order to enter into relationship with a spiritual reality which escapes the callow understanding of the cool, precise observer." This is the reason why it has been possible to fail so gravely to recognize this deeper personality in our exclusively scientific-minded civilization, and this disregard is the source of the present disorders in the world.

In mentally deranged persons, whose physical, psychic, and mental faculties are seriously impaired, there nevertheless "remains in the depths a real personality of unsuspected richness." Here is the proof that there is something else besides body, psyche, and mind.

These mentally ill persons, "even the most confused . . . have a fine feeling for another's strength or weakness, justice or arbitrariness, and are capable of judging very accurately the authority and respect possessed by a particular doctor, intern, or orderly. Equally well they sense what one thinks of them and they will be very sensitive, for example, to humiliations, lack of consideration, the slightest tactlessness, and above all to mockery and deception. So what appear to be the most disturbed manifestations of illness are actually means by which the spirit expresses and embodies itself."

Dr. Baruk identifies this deeper personality with the spirit which, hidden in the human heart, expresses itself through the body, the psyche, and the mind. It is the seat of "humane feeling," of the "sense of justice," of judgment concerning good and evil, of the conscience. "The deeper personality of our patients, like that of so-called normal people, is subject to the affectivity and the shocks of moral life with its interreactions of good and evil. Feelings of sympathy and antipathy, vexations, humiliations, pride, jealousy, suffering from injustice, yearnings for a better life, remorse, qualms of conscience, hatred, love—these are manifestations which are found in the depths of the sick person as well as in the normal person."

Moreover, this moral sensitivity can be exacerbated by illness, as I myself have observed, not in seriously mentally ill persons, but in the emotional, nervous, hypersensitive people who consult me day after day. They all feel with an almost incredible acuteness the slightest lack of sincerity, the slightest injustice, the least irritation shown toward them. And their reactions are such that they are constantly laying themselves open to fresh humiliations and stresses. So it is that if in a mental institution the doctor disregards the laws of this deeper personality and constantly resorts to forcible methods, such as confinement and cold baths, if he listens with only half an ear to the patients' complaints about unjust treatment, he only hurts them the more and increases their aggressiveness. This is conclusively shown in the experience of Dr. Baruk, who saw these manifestations of aggressiveness subside in the mentally ill in large measure when he imposed upon himself an absolute respect for the patient's personality and scrupulously forced himself to treat them justly in every least detail.

This mechanism is quite the same in the normal person. Dr. Baruk relates an incident in his military career. "We were assigned," he said, "to serve with North African natives who were in a state of extreme excitement and rebellion. A person who had previously been employed in this service, a self-styled expert in native affairs, declared when we arrived that the best way to deal with these people was a combination of deception and force. At the outset we found ourselves facing an attitude of hate and general hostility. All our attentions and attempts at appeasement were fruitless. Nevertheless, when we studied the question more deeply, we learned that these natives, who had fought courageously, were not treated on the same footing with the inhabitants of the capital (negligence with regard to their laundry, their food, their tobacco, disregard for their religious rules of diet, etc.). We then immediately took energetic measures to rectify these inequities and assure them of fair treatment. When they saw that something was actually being done for them, the attitude of these natives changed completely and their hostility gave way to a warm-hearted trust."

We see how the mechanism works: when the "person" is disregarded, when the importance of the spiritual personality is not recognized and the sense of humanity and justice is wounded, aggressive reactions are unleashed. Then all the conflicts which result provoke fresh acts of violence and multiply the injustices. At the same time we see how the problem of the person and the problem of the world are interrelated. If we ignore the spirit in our conception of man, then society, the state, industry, and science likewise ignore the spiritual needs of man. They wound man and thus bring about that flood of aggressive reactions and conflicts which go on increasing in a vicious circle. For everyone knows that here we are not dealing with a mechanism which is peculiar only to the sick or to "North African natives," but with a universal mechanism, a true explanation of our modern world where conflicts and injustices flourish together.

We have seen that medicine has lost the sense of the person. It would be easy now to show that the same thing is true in all the disciplines of our modern civilization. Dr. Stocker[33] remarks that the "great epochs" of human history have been those in which civilization has responded to the normal precedence of personhood. The primacy of the economic in the present epoch is the fundamental source of the social problem.

When René Lalive d'Epinay[50] instituted an inquiry into the social unrest among Swiss workers, one of them, a certain Herr Wagenknecht, replied: "There is a dignity in man. . . . he is not an 'individual' to exploit, but rather a 'person' to respect." I could quote here the discerning comments of Daniel Rops and many other authors on the depersonalization of industrialized society. And I ought also to mention the efforts of Emmanuel Mounier who has sketched the outlines of a "personalistic" society, and the work of Canon Boillat[51] in his book *La societé au service de la personne* ("Society in the Service of the Person").

The same is true in the area of law. Speaking of the crisis in law, Professor Kaegi[16] writes: "It is not a matter of re-establishing individualism but rather personalism."

With regard to art, I should like to quote Dr. Stocker again. He shows that the prerequisite of true art is an inner harmony and not a disharmony in the person of the artist. He writes, "G. K. Chesterton has quite rightly observed that 'the vigorous and healthy artists pour out their art as easily as they inhale and exhale.'" It is only "in shorter-winded artists that (this) function becomes an oppression and causes a definite suffering which is called the artistic temperament."

Hence, in order to heal society as well as to heal the patient, we must again see in man a person and restore the normal precedence which he lost through the repression of the spirit. Professor Jacques Ellul[52] has pointed out the complete failure of all present-day attempts to solve the political, economic, and social problems by way of purely technical methods. Conferences of experts multiply and the world's confusion only increases. For, he writes, "in our time the problems are primarily spiritual problems."

The healing of the disharmony of modern man, whether it be our sick persons or the whole of humanity, cannot be obtained solely through science. "From actual practice," writes Dr. Maeder,[2] "I have come to the conviction that an exclusively scientific approach does not suffice if one is to give the patient the maximum help which he expects and requires."

We have no intention of turning our back upon science and technology. We want only to make them more fruitful, to restore to them the normal precedence of personhood, which is to say, to subordinate them to the spirit. Just as the spirit gives meaning and life to our physiological and psychological functions, so it also gives to science and technology their proper place and significance. We want to fill the rift between the world of matter and the world of the spirit. "Prayer," writes Dr. de Rougemont,[11] "is a cure by silence, a necessary isolation, indispensable to the body as well as to thought. . . . To take our cross upon us is to accept the unity of body and spirit, to accept unseparated the inseparable whole in us."

We have seen that aggressiveness flourishes wherever injustice flourishes, that inevitably it seizes upon the countless people who are the victims of injustice in a civilization that no longer has any feeling for the person. But this is not all; the person who commits injustice, who violates and represses his conscience also conceals his bad conscience behind an aggressive exterior. This is the preventive offensive. "Contrary to what is generally believed," writes Dr. Baruk,[13] "the most intense and inexhautible conflicts that afflict mankind are far less the effect of excessive violence or the aggressive instinct than of a moral malaise. . . . The wild beast devours its victims without hating them, for the simple satisfaction of a need which disappears when it is satisfied. Moral malaise and unconscious guilt feelings, on the contrary, release vicious reactions of perversity and that particular form of refined and insatiable compulsion which we call hate." "None are so likely to become violent polemicists and to exhibit a violence, tenacity, and formidable dynamism, accompanied by denigration, accusation, and calumny, as those who have something on their conscience."

This, it appears to me, is the deeper explanation of our modern world and its disorders. In reaction to the abuses of the Middle Ages, in which the worst atrocities were committed in the name of spiritual values, the modern age has cast aside these values altogether. The great majority of our contemporaries in the countries of Western civilization live a physical, psychic, and mental life, but no longer live a conscious spiritual life. They feed their bodies, give free rein to feelings and their instincts, cultivate their intellect; but they no longer devote any time to the development of their spirit. They do not realize that the unleashing of conflicts, the hatreds, and the injustices of which they are constantly complaining are the grievous price they pay for this omission.

Governments tax their ingenuity in order to feed their people and satisfy their material needs; the universities educate people with conscientious care; the cinema provides abundant food for their imagination; but people remain restless and tormented. In the same way I have seen nervous people who suffer from what is called a complex of affective demands, that is, who from their childhood nurse the feeling that they have not been loved by their parents, always having received too little affection. Their parents, when told this, are dumfounded and indignant: "What do you have to complain about?" they reply; "you had everything you needed. We gave you a nice room and good food. We made sacrifices for your health and education." And, of course, this is true. But in the privacy of my office the patient goes on to say, "Yes, they gave me everything except what I needed most, an occasional caress, an occasional affectionate gesture, an unexpected gift at an unusual time, or one of those moments when parents really listen to their child in order to understand his troubles and anxieties, his hopes and his doubts, and his tormenting feeling of always being frustrated by himself."

The modern world has honestly decided to exclude everything emotional, moral, and religious. On November 10, 1619, in the course of a real mystical crisis, Descartes caught a glimpse of a new civilization in which men, in order to be able to tolerate themselves, would establish a science founded upon reason and common sense, a dependable science free from those moral value judgments which in his conviction had been the cause of all their previous controversies.

Thus the moral neutrality of science, and later that of the school, the economy, politics, and art, was proclaimed. Since that time, philosophy, religion, and poetry have been expelled from the real life of humanity. Very typical in this regard is the way in which Dr. Joseph Zwiebel[43] describes the world view he held before his conversion. It is much like that of the majority of our doctors today. "God, who possesses no objective reality, had no place in the universe"; he writes, "the divine was merely a creation of the human spirit. Hence, the world had no meaning in itself. So we human beings sought to give it a meaning. In searching for the meaning of the universe, we were finally able to give purpose to our world, our existence—but this purpose was merely subjective and purely human in origin. I denied all existence, every value of a transcendent order."

The reader may perhaps have felt that I was exaggerating in the first chapter when I described the repression of the spiritual. After all, are there still not philosophers, poets, and men of faith today, and very brilliant ones too? And despite the dominance of secularism and atheism, are not references sometimes made even in political assemblies to man's moral needs and to the commandments of God? Of course; I am by no means asserting that it has been possible to uproot faith, to despoil man of his yearning for the spiritual, to bolt and bar his conscience. But a *rift* has been effected. On the one side is the real life of mankind, dominated exclusively by material needs, instinctual reactions, intellect, by economics, science, and technology. And on the other side, ignored, kept under wraps, and ineffective, the world of the spirit—a tiny corner or sanctuary of the heart where one piously preserves the immortal spiritual values. Even if a scholar, an economist, or a politician makes some reference to spiritual things, this has only incidental importance in his discourse; one can see no connection between such a reference and the technical considerations that follow. It may be an altogether personal profession of faith which he respects, respects so much that it is no longer alluded to in the discussion of concrete problems. What characterizes our modern humanity, therefore, is not the absence of spiritual values—it possesses a spiritual elite, an abundance of faith and poetry—but rather the fact that these values no longer have any decisive influence upon the destiny of culture. They flourish in a beautiful garden where one escapes for a few moments, while the roads of political, economic, and cultural life remain bleak and barren thoroughfares. Even those who believe and go to church on Sunday and say their prayers at night, in their professional life, their family life, their practical life, their scientific activity subject themselves, like all the rest of the world, solely to the criteria of reason, to the interests and the technical rules which they have learned in a secularized school. And even we ourselves, who in growing numbers are seeking to put an end to this rift, we who declare that our faith is not concerned only with our personal salvation but must rather inspire us to find a more complete medical art, a more just economy, a more fruitful art, can testify day by day how deeply saturated we still are with this modern error. Often we still hesitate to search the Bible not only for the laws of our spiritual destiny, but also for the norms for the organization of society and the development of culture. Still there dwell in us two distinct men, whom we find it extremely hard to reconcile: the man of science who exercises his profession solely in the light of the objective knowledge which he acquired in the university, and the man of faith who does not reappear until the technician is left behind. There are many people of genuine faith who advocate with conviction this partitioning of life. They think that this fundamental distinction between the two domains, the spiritual and the practical life, is actually a necessary condition for the progress of science and technology: where would we be, they ask, if we were again to abandon the autonomy of thought? The result would be its strangulation by a philosophical system or a religious prejudice; again we would land in scholasticism or religious wars.

But these modern men, who fear a revival of the church, who, though they permit the church to concern itself with the spiritual life of its adherents, but fiercely forbid it to meddle with the culture or the political and economic life of man, these men nevertheless cherish a secret nostalgia for righteousness. They see very well that their civilization has not created the unanimity which Descartes envisioned; they feel a spiritual uneasiness, they are unhappy. More than once in my office I have talked with the man who is in revolt against the religion of his parents. With aggressive assurance he denounces all the harm that was done to him in his childhood by their moral formalism and their religious prejudices. He says he is an atheist. But when we go deeper, he finally admits his inner confusion, the dreadful void in which this skepticism has left him. He senses that a harmonious life and a real goal for his life cannot be found except by resorting to some higher power. And yet all these childhood memories keep him from doing this. His supreme grievance against his parents is that they disgusted him with religion. I have always had an immense sympathy with such souls who are imprisoned by inner conflict. What is being enacted in them is the tragedy of our present-day world.

Here, for example, is a young girl. She was raised by a very pious father, a church councilman who presided at meetings of his congregation and conducted daily family devotions. But his life in the family was a reign of terror; he beat his wife and tyrannized over his children in a shocking way. Every word about religion provoked in this young girl an immediate defensive reaction. Nevertheless, she assured me, she wanted to find her way back to the Christian faith because although her beliefs were so cruelly wounded by her father's behavior, at bottom she still believed in this faith. In the same way, in its childhood humanity saw the flaming stakes set afire by those whom Christ had sent to preach love to the world. Nevertheless, if humanity is outraged by every kind of torture, is it not perhaps because it is clinging to the message of love? And is not this fidelity, in spite of all the faults of the church, the best proof of the truth of Christianity?

Thus modern man appears to be disgusted with the religion for which he nevertheless feels a homesickness. He has repressed it, banished it from his life, proclaimed the exclusion of everything beyond the reach of the senses. He has consummated a great rift between the spiritual and the temporal world. And ever since, he has lived in a tragic duality.

The great schism in man's life manifests itself in two streams: the despiritualization of the world, on the one hand, and the disincarnation of the church, on the other. At the very time when the world wished to emancipate itself culturally and ethically from all moral or transcendent rules, the church withdrew within itself and lost its sense of reality. It talks about theology and psychology, feelings and doctrines, but no longer helps men in their real difficulties, of which it remains ignorant. It has fled into piety, into merely preaching salvation. Far be it from me to suggest that this is not its essential mission. But God also created the material world, not only the spiritual world. And the salvation he brings to us in Jesus Christ is not only the answer to the religious struggle of our souls, but also to the physical sufferings of the world. The language of the world and the language of the church have gone their separate ways, both with respect to content and to style. Magnificent sermons are preached in the church but the mass of men no longer come to hear them. They think the sermons are intended for the specialists who are preoccupied with theology. They do not expect from them anything that will contribute to the solution of the real problems of social, economic, and cultural life with which they have to grapple. Ministers—I know less about the Catholic church, but I suppose the priests also—appear to most men of our time to be idealists who have little understanding of practical life, who in any case cover up with pious phrases the cultural and social problems, the technical complexity of which they are quite unaware. "The church," a patient recently said to me, "stands outside of history."

Certainly, it is expected of statesmanship that it will restore justice, but this is expected to come only from the science of the expert and the technical perfection of the contracts which bind men. But, says Dr. de Rougemont, there are some "social contracts" which are free of "juridical inaccuracies" or "logical faults," but whose "impeccable system" nevertheless "secretes error." It is, of course, expected of the statesman or the economist that he will safeguard peace and security, but this expectation is applied only to his competence. His private life and religious ideas are not taken into account when he is elected to preside over the destiny of society. This is the dogma of the modern world which results from the schism between the spiritual and the temporal we have been talking about. Thus we allow divorced men and adulterers to work out laws for the protection of the family and appoint dubious business men, because of their experience, to sit in committees of economic experts. It is, however, "an established fact," writes Edouard Burnier,[53] "that public disorders have no other source except personal disorders."

"Religion is a private matter," said the Germans; but the whole modern world has adopted their slogan. The personal convictions of the politician, the artist, the scholar are not taken into consideration when their work is evaluated. This is the dream of *Realpolitik*, of art for art's sake, and of the autonomy of science.

"Science has misled us," writes Dr. Baruk, "into regarding the moral problems as useless." Even the scholars who are believers

have in all sincerity rallied to this idea that there is a fundamental demarcation between science and religion. "The two
domains are distinct," wrote Pasteur, "and woe to him who
would erase the boundary line between them."[54] Even in the
field of psychology and the psychology of religion, as Dr. Henri
Flournoy[55] declares, the exclusion of the transcendent is the
fundamental presupposition of scientific research. Science claims
that it is building up stone by stone a constantly developing
knowledge which necessarily sets it against metaphysical and
religious knowledge grounded upon fixed and eternal values.
"The great progress of modern thought," wrote Ernest Renan
in *L'avenir de la science*[56] ("The Future of Science"), "consisted
in substituting the category of becoming for the category of
being, the concept of the relative for the concept of the absolute,
of movement for immobility."

Today this scientific dogma is almost unanimously accepted.
A man can believe what he wishes; this is only his affair. But
as a scientific scholar, a builder of civilization he dare not give
any consideration whatever to his faith. He must confine himself exclusively to the ground of objectivity. Faith is the domain
of hypothesis which one can go on discussing forever. Only
objectivity leads to sure and effective knowledge.

There are five main objections which can be made to this
modern dogma:

1. Only a part of reality is accessible to objective knowledge;
it does not reach the essence of things. At the beginning of this
century, the great mathematician Henri Poincaré[57] demonstrated
that science by no means procures that indubitable knowledge
for which Descartes had hoped, that it is only a language, a
kind of algebra, a way of judging and drawing conclusions of
reason on the basis of a first assumption, which in itself is
just as hypothetical as all philosophical hypotheses. Science
does not select the most certain hypothesis, but rather the most
convenient hypothesis. Poincaré wrote: "The two propositions:

'the earth revolves' and 'it is more convenient to suppose that the earth revolves' mean one and the same thing; the one says no more than the other."[58]

Here the famous controversial question raised by Galileo, which we met with at the beginning of the rift between the spiritual and the temporal, is reduced by science itself to nothing! Science cannot prove absolutely that the earth revolves, but only that it revolves in relation to the whole universe. The church, on the other hand, has no reason to deny that the earth revolves. It is evident that basically the dispute is not intellectual but rather emotional. It is exactly like the quarrel between an adolescent and his parents, in which he scoffs at them by making assertions which are too categorical and they regard every contradiction on his part as an offense.

My teacher, the physicist, Charles-Eugène Guye,[59] was wont to repeat the words of a famous mathematician: "You draw from an equation only what you have put into it." This explains why those who assume that there is nothing spiritual in man never in fact encounter the spirit. In their observations they note only the physico-chemical data and in the end they have only a physico–chemical explanation of the phenomena. But this is only a description of the mechanism of the phenomena and not of their cause, a picture of their reciprocal relationships but not of their nature.

2. True objectivity does not exist. It is impossible to eliminate the observer. This was established by Werner Heisenberg in the formulation of his principle of indeterminacy.[8] At a certain stage, that of classical science, one can still labor under an illusion, for the margin of indeterminacy inherent in the instrument of observation is relatively negligible in relation to the observed facts. But now that we have reached the stage of modern physics, the stage of nuclear physics, this margin of indeterminacy does not appear to be so negligible and in any case must be taken into account. Nothing is more revealing of the relative character of

science; for what at one stage appears to be certain, at another is no longer so. "It is the stage that creates the phenomenon," wrote Guye.[59]

3. We know, however, that modern physics has gone much further. At the nuclear stage pheonomena can be envisaged either as bodies or as wave movements: ". . . two points of view which at first appear irreconcilable, but which in reality never come into direct conflict."[8] This is Niels Bohr's principle of complementarity. It throws our classical concept of matter into question. Matter, then, is perhaps only the form in which we see the spirit. "The stuff of the world is the stuff of the spirit," writes the physicist Eddington.[38]

4. On the other hand, the exclusion of faith has neither logical nor experimental foundation. It is a philosophical *a priori* and therefore is not scientific. In a penetrating study Dr. Tzanck[23] shows that at least in human biology we must necessarily appeal to faith as much as to knowledge. We do this without accounting for it and thus permit ourselves to think that we are respecting the scientific dogma of the exclusion of faith. However, we have no means, for example, of "knowing" whether a person other than ourselves is endowed with consciousness. We can only assume it, and that means to believe it, to rely upon his testimony and his introspection. "Faith," writes Dr. Tzanck, "has its legitimate place in science, and especially in the biological sciences." And Dr. Ponsoye says the same: The central fact which is overlooked by the mechanists is that knowing includes believing and is conditioned by it.[38]

As a matter of fact this claim of science to exclude faith in order to base itself solely upon knowing has led to an intellectual enfeeblement of modern man. Bergson showed this when he pointed out the pre-eminent importance of intuition for all fruitful thinking. And Dr. Tzanck writes: "Intuition relates to consciousness in the realm of believing, whereas intelligence relates to consciousness in the realm of knowing."

The great ambition of positivism, when it relegated morality, religion, and aesthetics to the purely subjective and attempted to build knowledge solely upon objective knowing, was therefore a mere utopia. "In the objective method," writes Dr. Baruk, "the observer studies the phenomena from the outside, without participating in any way in the inner life that animates them. . . . With this method how can one ever comprehend the deeper feelings that motivate the individual and entire societies?"[13]

5. And finally, the noncommitment of the scientist is also a utopia. That the work of science is morally neutral, that the man of science must pursue his studies without any thought of their moral repercussions—until a few years ago this was almost universally recognized. But now that the atom bomb is charged with such great material explosive force we can say that it has brought about a no less grave moral and spiritual explosion in the scientific world. The public still does not realize what a formidable repercussion it had upon the scientists. "Will they," asks Louis de Broglie, "every time they begin a project, ask themselves whether they have the right in the face of all humanity to pursue research which sooner or later may lead to unheard-of catastrophes?"[1] And the physicist André George replies, "The scientist dare not on the one hand say: Everything that is valuable and important in the history of man is owing to me, and at the same time say: I have nothing to do with our catastrophes; these are the fault of others."[1]

Anybody can judge the import of such reflections. For in the thought of the last century the moral neutrality of the scientist was the prerequisite of scientific progress and the progress of science was the prerequisite for the happiness of mankind. Now the scientist suddenly becomes aware that by his very desire to be neutral he has ceased to be neutral, that he has made himself an accomplice of evil, an accessory of the forces which destroy the welfare of humanity.

"Science," writes George, "may perhaps stand above morality as well as art. But not the scientist . . . the scientist too is committed."

As we see, it is the men of science themselves who today are attacking from all angles the fundamental postulate upon which modern science is based, namely, that there is a water-tight wall between the world of the spirit (philosophy, morality, and faith) and the world of matter (science and objective knowledge). The mathematicians through their critical study of scientific reasoning, the physicists through their research into the structure of matter, the biologists through their reflections upon the mystery of life—all of them, through observing the disquieting historical results connected with the great myth of the blessings of science, are asking the same questions: Was this rift between the moral domain and the material and intellectual domain really justified? Could one, without selling out to evil and impotence, brush aside the world of "values," as one had for three centuries sincerely believed one must do?

For that is indeed the postulate of the Renaissance on which modern civilization is built.

True, even before the Renaissance there were brutal, immoral, and heretical people. And after the Renaissance there were poets, thinkers, and saints. But this is not the question. There have always been and always will be in man impulses which prompt him to reject the laws of the spirit and repress the conscience which is the echo of those laws in his heart. But up to the time of the Renaissance nobody contested the supremacy of these laws of the spirit, even when they violated or gropingly pursued their research. Nobody denied that these were "values," that is, realities which were created neither by the hand nor by the brain of man, truths which surpassed man, truths which he could handle dialectically, but which he could not leave out of consideration. One could have differing views of these values but not of the idea of value itself.

Since the Renaissance, humanity in the intoxication of its adolescence has contested this idea.

Since that time there have been three possible attitudes, which we shall now consider in this order: one can send these values off on vacation; one can fabricate new values; or one can deny that they exist.

1. Values on vacation. This, as we have seen, is the attitude of modern science. It does not deny the supersensible; it sends it off on a holiday. It studies the world as if these supersensible values were absent and played no part in it. We need not discuss this further.

This is also the attitude of the secularists. They tolerate the church, provided that it keeps quiet in its own little corner and does not presume to meddle in the real life of the world, in education, politics, and economics. They propose to build these things upon the foundation of complete neutrality, moral and religious. They appeal to a "secular morality" which has no other source except the scientific study of society, which they undertake to set in order. I have already mentioned Sartre's[3] pertinent criticism of this secular morality. This philosopher has shown how fragile and inconsistent this first attitude is. If one wants to send these values on vacation and live as if they did not exist, then logically one must one day deny them and live as one pleases.

Liberalism too takes this attitude. The bigwig of free economy makes a great to-do about values. Often he is a pious man who may even be concerned about the spiritual welfare of his employees. But for him this spiritual realm has no connection with economic life, which is regulated only by the material laws of competition and needs. I often wonder how these liberals can applaud the personalistic social doctrines and sincerely claim that there is nothing new in them, since they have always applied and the human person has always been sacred in their eyes. But what they lack, without knowing it, is the sense of incarnation. For the spirit, which they reverence, is inseparable from the body; one cannot honor the spirit without also subjecting to it man's economic life.

Finally, it is also the attitude of the literary liberalism which is so characteristic of our age, that of André Gide, for example, and his theme of "availability" (*disponibilité*), "his aversion to committing himself, his refusal to limit himself," as Paul Archambault[1] puts it. Values must be sent on vacation, locked up in a cupboard in order that one may taste everything unhindered as long as one is sincere. We know the despair to which this attitude led Gide. "I assure you," he wrote, "that the feeling of freedom can plunge the soul into a kind of anguish." "Give me some reason for living. I have none left. I have freed myself. That may be. But what does it signify? This objectless liberty is a burden to me."[60]

2. Fabricated values. If it is possible to furlough values and live as if they did not exist, it is also possible to adopt new ones; one can concoct one's own values. This second attitude is that of Nietzsche: "All goals have been destroyed. Men must give themselves a goal. It was an error to believe that they had one; they chose all their own goals." We must become "murderers of God" in order to put new values in his place, such as the "Superman" or the "will to power." Certainly Nazism did not come directly out of Nietzsche. Nietzsche detested the state and despised German nationalism. But once one fabricates some values one can also fabricate others, such as race and the historic mission of Germany, which goes back to Hegel. And the crossbreeding of Nietzsche's and Hegel's values produced Nazism. Moreover, Nietzsche himself foresaw this: "Contemporary Europe . . . has no suspicion whatever that, thanks to me, a catastrophe is preparing, whose name I know, but which I will not tell."[1]

Science likewise has fabricated values (this science which has claimed that it can get along without them)—notably the value called "progress," which we shall discuss in the next chapter.

3. We come now to the end of the development which began with the Renaissance. Only in the course of the last century did men dare to draw the logical conclusion from the great rift of modern times. If one can disregard values, then one ends by denying them. This is the attitude of Marx, Sartre, and Freud.

We know the communistic doctrine: religion is only "opium for the people," a human invention that serves the capitalist powers. Economic laws and necessities are the sole determinants of history. "The relationship which appears to us to be fundamental," writes the Communist theoretician Pierre Hervé,[1] "is the relation between man and the universe. . . . Man must live in dependence upon the planet on which he finds himself. . . . This relationship is not speculative, but practical; it is a relationship that is established through a material activity; and this relationship is not individual, but collective." Here we have the two dogmas of Communism: there is only a material and a collective reality.

This is also the attitude of Sartre: "Existentialism is nothing else but an attempt to draw the full conclusions from a consistently atheistic position." But in a way that is hardly logical he adds, "Even if God existed that would make no difference."[3] There could not be a clearer avowal that the "atheistic position" is a basic principle. But Sartre runs into a difficulty similar to that of Gide: "The existentialist," he says, "finds it extremely embarrassing that God does not exist, for there disappears with Him all possibility of finding values in an intelligible heaven." Elsewhere he says, "My freedom is the sole foundation of values, and nothing, absolutely nothing, justifies my adopting a particular value, this or some other scale of values. . . . And my freedom is afraid of being the foundationless foundation of values." And in another place he says, "I am condemned to be free." We can therefore understand his callous cynicism about man: ". . . this obscene and empty existence is bestowed upon him in vain." For without God one can no longer understand man. "A philosophy of nothingness," says Gabriel Marcel.[1]

And finally, it is the attitude of Freud. I mean by this his philosophical teaching. Though we are grateful to him for his scientific work, we must recognize, on the other hand, that there is no necessary connection between his scientific contributions and the philosophical views which he believed he must deduce from it. In his scientific work he was a genius who cast a brilliant light upon the psychological mechanisms that occur in the unconscious, what his disciple, Dr. Charles Odier[49] calls "functions," as distinguished from "values." And yet subsequently he maintained that all spiritual values, religion, morality, poetry, are to be reduced to these functions. The conscience, he wrote, "is obviously an anxiety unleashed by the risk of not being loved, a 'social' anxiety."[61] In this way Freud came to deny all value, which prompts Gustave Thibon to say, "Marx and Freud are brothers."[18] God, the good, the beautiful are nothing more than projections of affective states, rationalizations of instinctual psychic functions. This attitude is so difficult to uphold that a genuine Freudian, like Dr. Odier,[49] has come to admit that there are "two sources of moral life: the functions (which for Freud are the exclusive source) and the values (which Freud denied). I have asked myself whether this further development of Freud's doctrine was exceptional. Recently, however, I was invited to a group of Freudian psychoanalysts and I asked them quite frankly: "Is there a single one of you who still adheres to Freud on this point of reducing all values to psychic functions?" The response was unanimously negative, and one of the doctors present added that to be true to Freud one must continue on the road of objective observation of man which he opened up for us, and that this would mean recognizing that values play a role in the life of man's soul which is independent of his functions, if observation shows us that this is the case.

Thus we see that in every sector this rift which opened up since the Renaissance leads us into a blind alley. Whether it be science and its claim to assure the happiness of mankind by setting aside the spiritual realities; or the intellectual freedom advocated by Gide and Sartre; or Nietzsche's attempt to show that there are no values at all, we find nothing but contradictions, anxiety, and catastrophe.

I am not presenting here a bill of indictment. I want to guard against adopting a tone of triumph or posing as a partisan and speaking in the name of believers, who would cry out to the world in its distress: "It serves you right; you should have listened to us!" No, our faith prescribes love for our fellow men, and for ourselves an honest recognition of our own faults. Our faith demands that we understand the man of our time, not that we accuse him. We can well understand why modern man, tired of a misused guardianship on the past of the church and disillusioned by all sorts of excesses committed in the name of spiritual values, has honestly searched for new ways. First he tried to eliminate these spiritual things which have been the subject of so much controversy. Then inevitably he was led to the point of trying to organize the world as if these values were nonexistent; and today he is dying of spiritual undernourishment. "An illness which is widespread in modern times," writes Dr. Maltarello,[42] "is the absence of inwardness."

For this historic error we believers too are clearly responsible. The church has withdrawn, it has not been interested in the real world. It offered to the world nothing but a purely spiritual bread which no longer satisfies its hunger.

Perhaps this historic error was a necessary crisis, like that of an adolescent before he works out an integration. However, what will be needed to put an end to the rift will be a return to the self, on the part of the church as well as the world.

Now, we shall be able to judge the extent of this spiritual undernourishment if we look at all these movements from another angle: not as errors but rather as attempts to find healing. I use this comparison: For a long time medical men combated fever as if it itself constituted the illness. Medicine today inclines rather to respect it, not only as a symptom of the disease but of the struggle of the organism against the disease. True, it is this struggle which makes it ill, and yet this very struggle is also the proof of its vitality and is the necessary way to healing. Likewise, we can regard Communism, Nazism, existentialism, or Freudianism as symptoms of a profound illness of the world, but also as signs of its reaction against this illness.

The modern schism between the spiritual and the temporal, of which we have been speaking, has deprived man of a nourishment which he needs. He has been told that the spirit is a superfluous hypothesis which he can well do without. He has been exhorted to throw overboard the naïve faith of his ancestors along with their ancient prejudices. He has been assured that reason and positive knowledge are sufficient for his life; that he can live by bread alone. But he has such a great need for faith that he, being robbed of his faith in the true God, has alternately and in most naïve fashion put his faith in the new gods, in science, in the Superman or the victory of the proletariat.

A passage from Sartre is symptomatic in this connection: "All kinds of materialism lead one to treat every man including oneself as an object—that is, as a set of pre-determined reactions, in no way different from the patterns of qualities and phenomena which constitute a table, or a chair or a stone. Our aim is precisely to establish the human kingdom as a pattern of values distinct from the material world."[3] Here is the champion of atheism confessing that it is his aim to conquer materialism; here is the negator of values avowing that he wishes to restore a peculiarly human value!

Seen from this point of view, all of these characteristic movements of the modern world appear to be worthy of our full sympathy. For they are, as it were, the living proof that man cannot dispense with the spirit. The attempt is made to deprive him of it; so he invents surrogates for it. He has been urged not to talk any more about God; so he expresses his spiritual yearnings in camouflaged forms. In Communism he seeks less an economic doctrine than a substitute for love. In science he seeks less a material power than a substitute for knowledge. In Nazism he seeks less a political power than a substitute for mysticism; in existentialism less a skepticism than a substitute for humanism;

in psychoanalysis a substitute for confession and salvation, and —as far as religious people are concerned—in formalism a substitute for justification by faith. Since science has lost its crown, since it has been cut off from the spiritual source of all true knowledge, it has sought feverishly and insatiably for new knowledge. Since men have wished to murder God, the multitudes have been running after all the ideologies that claim to bring them values that surpass man. Since men have been playing the freethinker and man of reason, who has no truck with sentiment, man appears in all his distress to be a plaything of fear. "He is ready to throw himself into the arms of any religion," says Jacques Ellul, "in order to fill up the void left by Christianity."[52]

Therefore all these movements in our contemporary world appear as just so many Messianisms. Take science: even Descartes regarded his philosophy in a Messianic sense when he envisaged it as being founded upon an "indubitable knowledge." "Descartes," wrote Bergson, "created an attitude of spirit which imposed itself upon philosophy as well as science. . . . an unlimited confidence in the power of intelligence."[62] And yet it was not until the last century that this Messianic note was affirmed with an air of triumph: "Every man who can read is a saved man," wrote Eugène Manuel. How man thirsts for salvation! At that time man's corruption was attributed to his emotions and passions, and against these were marshalled public education and reason. But now Moréas says, "If there are passions, then reason is one of them, and one of the most intemperate of all."[19]

Ernest Renan wrote his *L'avenir de la science* ("The Future of Science")[56] with all the passion of a prophet. He publicly proclaimed himself the priest of a new religion: science. "Science alone," he said, "can ameliorate the unhappy situation of man here below." His program was to organize humanity scientifically. Hippolyte Taine likewise spoke of "the religion of science." Alas, what a different tune we must sing today about these rash hopes!

But now technology has put its mirage in the place of the *Fata Morgana* of the science from which it emerged. Great nations tremble in veritable mystical transport in the planning of an industrialization carried to its limits. It is also a kind of technological mysticism which characterizes a whole literature of psychoanalysis which would make of this discipline not only a therapeutic procedure but the instrument of a veritable liberation of man.

I hardly need to point out the Messianic significance of Nietzsche's work and the Nazi tragedy.

This is also the place to mention the naturist Messianism of Jean-Jacques Rousseau. "The threefold Christian doctrine of man, who came from the hands of Providence in a state of goodness, was corrupted by sin, and restored through grace," writes René Gillouin,[19] "was replaced by Jean-Jacques . . . with another, completed self-invented triad, that of man who came from nature in a state of goodness, was corrupted by society, and restored by returning to nature."

And finally, that which gave the Marxist proclamation influence upon the masses was also a mere myth, whose mystical power, as Gillouin describes it, "is a faith in the Messianic calling of the proletariat."[19]

So for those who have eyes to see there is a terrible yearning in our modern world, an inner torment to which all these movements and their ephemeral success bear witness. This world has repressed the spiritual, but the point is that it has *only* been able to repress it; at the bottom of its heart it still has a yearning for it. Freud has taught us that an idea or an emotion which is repressed returns to the consciousness in disguised form. The disguise has succeeded: the life of the spirit has reappeared in the form of economic doctrines, atheistic philosophy, and scientific materialism. It is thus a spiritual faith that lends weight to all these theories.

Consider what happened under the Nazi dominion. In a Germany where there would certainly have been a cry of clericalism if the church had attempted to influence politics, culture, art, medicine, and law, an ideology which penetrated all of these disciplines was able to triumph. I, for my part, believe that, if it was able not only to penetrate but to enslave them, this was possible because in spite of everything men cherish a secret longing to fill the rift which the modern schism has created between the spiritual and the temporal.

The true problems of men are metaphysical, religious, and emotional in character. They are the problems which the physician discovers today in the tormented souls who come to consult him in ever greater numbers. They are dread, the fear of death, remorse, and the thirst for love and forgiveness. Even though they are hardly conscious of these things any longer, the great mass of people today are suffering from nothing less than this. Neither science, which is mute in the face of the irrational, nor liberalism, which is indifferent to the need for human fellowship, nor socialism, which is blind to sin, have any answer to these questions.

There is nothing more eloquent in this regard than the present development in Russia. Father Boisselot[1] tells us that when Paul Nizan returned from Soviet Russia, Nizan said to him: "At the present time there is in Russia one problem, and it is a problem of the inner life, the moral life. As long as the heroic phase of the Revolution lasted, heroism took the place as it were of morality and it galvanized all emotions. But now that this has almost subsided the eternal questions reappear. . . . In all the meetings, in all the student circles what are young men and young women discussing? Love, suffering, and death. We cannot hide from this holy trilogy; they constantly thrust themselves upon us." Father Boisselot adds: "And now what would they propose? The answer that Nizan gave was Stoicism. Stoicism, for an entire people, is not very convincing to me; whereas we, precisely because of our distinctive conception of the cross, are able to amalgamate all these things in our conception of the world, this whole domain of the inner life, the psychic life, the emotional life, which are so incredibly neglected by modern man."

Therefore the present age appears to us to be the final crisis of modern times, which are characterized by a schism between the spiritual and the temporal. Tired of partial solutions, tired of material progress which does not deliver it from its spiritual anguish, tired of intellectual dialectics which never become incarnate in real life, humanity yearns for the recovery of a unitary conception of man and the world. Since it is still not willing to return to the Christianity from which it has been estranged for several centuries, it plunges desperately into all kinds of contradictory ideologies which claim to be able to solve the problem. After trying so many false solutions, will it finally be able again to embrace the true one?

The reader may perhaps be offended by what I have just said. By what right do I declare the Christian solution the true solution? I leave to the theologians their task, which is to give an apologetic argument for this. I shall remain on my own ground, which is that of psychology. I have shown that, despite his revolt against Christianity, modern man at the bottom of his heart actually cherishes a Christian ideal. This at least justifies us in affirming that a return of our civilization to its Christian sources constitutes the one true solution. In the last analysis this is a matter of faith and not of logical demonstration.

But will our Christian churches be capable of responding to this confused yearning of the modern world? It is clear that they cannot simply insist upon a *"mea culpa,"* a repentant return to the fold. Just as the parents of our rebellious adolescent cannot expect him to become a child again and submit to their spiritual tutelage, so the church cannot dream of nullifying the intellectual and temporal emancipation of our modern society. After the tyrannical domination the church perpetrated upon society, after entering into the expedient of the separation of church and state, it will certainly be necessary to find a new harmony between the church and society, between the spirit and the body.

This we shall deal with in the last chapter of this book. But before we do this we must examine two of the great dogmas of modern times: the myth of progress and the myth of power. They will help us to gain a better understanding of the spiritual drama of our time. At the very time when science claimed that it had finally overthrown the ancient beliefs and put an end to the mythological age of mankind, humanity, without knowing what it was doing, created new myths.

CHAPTER IV

The Myth of Progress

[IT WAS MORE than fifteen years ago that I wrote this book. In the meantime, science has greatly developed—and so have I! Less young as I am today, I would hesitate to plunge so naïvely into a field in which I lack competence in such a way that specialists in paleontology would be able to point out errors in this chapter. However, they will grant, I hope, that I was not claiming to develop a scientific doctrine here. My only concern was to present an essay on the more or less conscious role which the emotions and the philosophical ideas of an age play in the minds of scientists, despite their efforts to be critical and objective. However, without realizing it, I was putting into these pages more emotion and subjectivity than was proper and of which I keep seeking to divest myself with advancing age.

The development of the science of anthropology has followed exactly the same pattern. After the enthusiastic and oversimplified flights of the first transformists, the science subjected itself to a criticism of its own doctrines which was more and more severe and more humble. Important new discoveries were also made in Java and Peking. But above all, innumerable studies in America as well as in Europe have been devoted to determining, with respect to our ideas about the evolution of the world and the species, what can be retained as established fact and what must be abandoned as being mere seductive intellectual opinions. Only the specialists are capable of sifting out these facts. Thus there can be no question of my attempting now to correct this chapter in the light of studies which I have not been able to pursue. In my incompetence I would only multiply the errors.

I may point out, however, that the development of scientific thought on this subject has actually passed through this same process of critical revision of which I was then expressing the hope that it would occur. As an example, I mention only the work of Père Pierre Teilhard de Chardin. Though written by a scientist, it is now so well known by the general public beyond scientific circles that I cannot fail to cite it. Père Teilhard is dealing with a doctrine of evolution, but he himself carefully distinguishes this from transformism, which he calls an "old hypothesis . . . decrepit." The evolution of the world—as Père Teilhard sees it and which for him is "prolonged" to include the social evolution of man and his "personalization"—is "directed" by and towards an "Omega point" which he declares to be "preëxistent and transcendent" to creation. We see here a conception of evolution which has been completely stripped of the three philosophical notions which I denounced in this chapter: accident, struggle, and progress.

Moreover, he makes two insertions in his scientific view, not only in the future ahead, at the end of the world, when, as St. Paul says, God will be "all in all," but also in the past, at the origin of the world. For him the universe always has two aspects, an aspect of matter and an aspect of "consciousness," the "without" and the "within" of things. As a man of science, he is careful not to employ the classical terms "physical" and "metaphysical," but this is the question which I am raising here, namely, that of a unified conception of the world, a solution of the schism between matter and spirit.

As Teilhard de Chardin himself has shown, such views of evolution are in accord with the given fundamentals of Christian revelation. Naturally, they raise many questions of detail, but on the whole they are on the side of a reconciliation between science and religion, which is the central theme of this present book and one which is as close to my heart today as it was in 1947.—P.T., February, 1964.]*

I beg the reader not to take too seriously every word in this chapter. In the midst of the grave problems that demand our concern we must be able to smile a bit too. In order that we may not take ourselves too seriously, it is good for us to be able to indulge in a kindly smile at the attacks of naïve enthusiasm which sometimes seize the minds of even the most serious of men. The extraordinary history of the myth of progress constitutes for us a salutary lesson in humility. It shows us how small man remains, despite all his discoveries and inventions, in the face of the mystery of the universe. These pose more problems than they solve. And men have such a hunger to believe something that, once they are carried away by enthusiasm, they soon forget the much touted scientific doubt and the celebrated common sense on which they thought they wanted their new civilization to be founded.

Faith in progress is the thought which is latent in our whole modern world. At the same time that men wanted to make short shrift of religious faith in the name of reason, faith in progress spread so universally that up until recently no one dreamed of questioning it.

The gospel had brought to humanity a great hope. It was the hope that salvation would descend from heaven, that God would intervene in history, transform men's hearts, and save them from their misery more surely than all their clever calculations; and finally the hope of the triumphant return of Christ, who in the course of his earthly ministry had given glorious proof of his power and love through his death and resurrection.

The repression of the Christian faith of which we have spoken, would perhaps have plunged humanity into despair, if it had not

* The author has supplied these prefatory comments for this English version. The references to Teilhard de Chardin are in the main to the latter's book *The Phenomenon of Man* (New York: Harper & Row, 1959). (Trans.)

been supported by this new faith that salvation would rise up from the earth itself. A delusive faith to be sure, but one which nevertheless stirred up in countless scholars a marvelous devotion. Almost all of us believe in it, despite the fact that history gives the lie to it.

For the biblical myth, according to which man through this disobedience forfeited his destiny and was redeemed by God who gave his life to bring him back to Himself, the modern world has substituted the myth of progress—the myth that man was born of inert matter by accident and by his own intelligence is slowly elevating himself toward perfection.

This new myth was therefore bound up with the mythical faith in science of which we have already spoken. And again at its birth we meet Descartes, enthusiastically describing his vision that "if a majority of men would join their life and their work, all of us together would get farther than each one by himself could do."

This myth took shape in the eighteenth century among the philosophers, Condorcet and Volney in particular, and triumphed universally in the nineteenth century. I have cited Renan who said of himself, "I, the priest of the true religion" and went on to say, "My religion is always the progress of reason, that is, science."[56] One could not avow more clearly that the purpose, as Renan affirmed, was not to overthrow religion and substitute science for it, but rather to replace the Christian religion with a new religion. When positivism so paradoxically crowns its rational structure with its cult of the "Unknowable" it likewise admits that what we have here is really a theological debate and not a scientific one. Humanity, writes Teilhard de Chardin, "has literally converted to a species of religion . . . [a] passionate faith in the value and the potentialities of human effort."[1]

But what gave to the myth of progress its final consecration was the ideas of Darwin. A myth is not a particular theory; it is a general conception which can be applied to all domains. It must contain an explanation of the world. It was precisely

Descartes' idea to renounce all premature general explanations and wait until a slowly rising edifice of knowledge, built upon one sure fact after another, would lead to such a general explanation. But when Darwin appeared on the scene with a new explanation of the world which conformed with the prevailing faith, this waiting attitude was quickly forgotten. With overflowing enthusiasm a few paleontological discoveries were hastily generalized and proclaimed as definitive proof of the doctrine. It was evolutionism more than any other scientific theory popularized the idea that the world is progressing in a meaningful development which proceeds from primitive imperfection to final perfection. We shall therefore examine more closely this doctrine of evolution, which still today remains the foundation of instruction in natural science in our schools.

What it was that won the world to Darwin's doctrines was not the already well-known idea of a homogeneous continuity between various species of living beings, from the simplest to the most highly developed, but rather the idea of a plausible mechanism of descent. We must allow that our minds are pleased to be able to trace back the extreme diversity of animal species to one original form and we can well understand the haste with which Darwin's views were adopted. And yet there is another reason for this acceptance, and it is the true reason for Darwin's success: along with the hypothesis of "natural selection" he provided an explanation of the progressive diversification of species, an explanation which had no need for God, since, after all, everything happened by law.

We know, however, that Darwin was a believer and that in the first edition of *The Origin of Species* he spoke of God as the director of this whole evolution. His book, however, had such great success and was received with such enthusiasm by the German materialists, and especially by Huxley, that Darwin, intoxicated with success, hastened to cut out God in the second edition. Actually, the doctrine can get along without Him, and therein lay the deeper cause of its triumph. We know Darwin's theory: it presupposes that at any moment and by pure accident new characteristics may arise in a given species. It presupposes further that of all these innumerable new varieties only those survive which are more fit than the others to prevail in the struggle for existence. In this way progress occurs automatically without any need for a God to effect it.

Thus Darwin's doctrine gave to the world a new trinity: progress, accident, and struggle. Accident ultimately leads to progress, thanks to the universal struggle.

Once enthusiasm has been let loose it keeps right on going. If accident and struggle explain the progress of living species and reduce them to unity, then they must also explain the transition from the inanimate world to the animate world and reduce the whole world to unity. What a grand vision! Doubtless it was accident that one day a particular combination of atoms came together to form an albuminous molecule, found that it was alive, and subsequently was able to engender all the vegetable and animal species. A bold extrapolation, which, it is true, serious scholars never ventured to put forward as a certainty, but which is nevertheless so pleasing that today the whole world believes it, thanks, I dare say, to the benefit of doubt. As long as it is expressly declared that the descent of the species through natural selection is "proved by science," it may be hoped that science will some day also prove the fortuitous transformation of inanimate matter into animate matter.

All this constitutes a movement of thought so powerful that it has even won over the believers in God. I recently read a dissertation by a French Catholic physician, Dr. Guy Trolliet,[63] who takes great pains to bring this materialistic explanation of the world into accord with the biblical revelation, which it most obviously contradicts. Trolliet goes so far as to find in St. Augustine and St. Thomas precursors of the doctrine of evolution!

However, he finally runs up against creation of man, where a reconciliation of the two becomes problematic. As a matter of fact, if Darwin's doctrine is extrapolated to explain the transition from the inorganic world to the animate world, Darwin himself had already extended it to the transition from animal to man and claimed to explain the formation of man by natural selection. Thus man, far from being the fruit of a special creation, as the Bible expressly says, would have derived accidentally from an ape which had accidentally acquired new characteristics which favored erect carriage and the birth of conscience. Dr. Trolliet coolly declares: "A mutation gave rise to man!"

Finally, this view of evolutionary progress is applied to the history of man, who has slowly elevated himself from obscure origins to the victory of his clear intelligence. Dr. M. Engelson[64] has stated the doctrine of the three eras of humanity generally held today as follows: "animistic, naïve religious, scientific."

Our whole contemporary world is saturated with this concept, this myth of an upward march of the world from the first electron through the first living cell to the first conscious man, who will now lead humanity to a marvelous future, to which it is being automatically steered by these same "laws" of evolution. If there are still many imperfections and injustices in the world, just wait awhile. The golden age will come, it is just ahead of us; it will be brought about through the interplay of accident and struggle. The golden age was not at the beginning, as the Bible asserts; the present world is not the result of a disordering of an original perfection, but is rather a progress from primitive chaos, a march toward unlimited progress.

This is the official doctrine which is taught to our children in school. What is dubious about this is that it is not presented to them as a purely philosophical hypothesis—after all, philosophy has been repressed; the pretense is that all philosophizing has ceased!—but rather as a truth which is solidly based upon scientific discoveries.

Today, however, the doctrine of transformation has been shaken by a number of facts. Far from being a scientific truth, it is being challenged at many points by scientific discoveries. It is encountering four major objections:

First, those of paleontology, which was once its cradle. Paleontology, the science of fossils which in Darwin's time was still in its infancy, as it has developed has thrown into question various expressions of the doctrine of evolution. It is clear that, if things had happened exactly as this theory says they did, then one would have to find the fossils of animals which are less developed than ours in the oldest strata which have been explored. But now Professor Maurice Caullery,[65] one of the most authoritative protagonists of the official doctrine of transformation, writes: "In the Cambrian period, the first from which we possess fossils in any abundance, the animal kingdom already presents a physiognomy which does not differ essentially from that of our present world." I could multiply the quotations; for these are matters which are recognized by the most fervent evolutionists. Moreover, Caullery honestly adds, "Actually, every type may have existed for long periods before that in which we find them for the first time."

We have seen that paleontology in the course of its development has found in the primitive strata not only primitive animals but more and more fossils of more highly developed animals. C. Depéret[66] writes: "The more our paleontological discoveries accumulate the farther back in time does the first appearance of each large group of animal fossils, even those in the most highly developed zoological stages, retreat."

The adherents of transformism are therefore obliged to assume that the descent of species, as conceived by Darwin, occurred in an epoch so remote that paleontology cannot furnish us with adequate documentation of it. A very gratuitous supposition, to be sure, since, lacking documentation, it escapes all scientific verification. Georges Salet and Louis Lafont can therefore conclude that ". . . the paleontological facts are exactly the opposite of that which the doctrine of transformism led us to expect."[58]

The second class of objection relates to the independence of the large animal groups. Darwin's doctrine actually presupposed not only a descent of species within these groups but also between the various branches of the animal kingdom. We know the fervor with which the scientists launched into the search for transitional types which would confirm these views. But it was in vain. "The major part of the fundamental types of the animal kingdom," writes Depéret,[66] "appear to us to have no connection whatsoever from a paleontological point of view." And with the same honesty which I pointed out before, the spokesman for transformism, Maurice Caullery, recognizes this: "The great lines of the animal kingdom," he writes, "are already drawn in the most ancient epochs, and the various groups are separated from one another by discontinuities of the kind which we find today."[65]

We still remember the fuss that was made over the *archeopteryx* (the fossil primitive bird), which the evolutionists wished to regard as a transitional type between the reptiles and the birds. But if we look at it more closely and without prejudice it must be admitted that it has all the specific characteristics of the reptiles and none of those of the birds. It is a reptile that resembles a bird and resembles it even less than does a bat.

Third, Darwin's doctrine presupposes the hereditary transmission of acquired characteristics. Quite evidently, this is the *conditio sine qua non* of the theory. For in order that one species may transform itself into another it is not sufficient that an individual acquire a new character "by accident"; it must also transmit it to its descendants. But here again all the furious research of scientists, observers, and experimental breeders over the last century has remained inconclusive. Jean Rostand, the materialistic biologist and advocate of transformism, writes quite frankly: "The facts forbid us to believe in the inheritance of physical modifications."[17] "Everything proceeds," writes Dr. Tzanck,[23] "as if living beings were capable of acquiring new characteristics and transmitting them to their descendants. . . . But now we not only find no irrefutable proof whatsoever for such natural transformations, but also when we seek experimentally to create mutilations upon organisms we never succeed in obtaining any that are hereditarily transmissible."

Indeed, science even undertook to make us understand why this is so when Naegeli, and after him Weismann, introduced into biology the fundamental distinction between germ plasm (*germen*) and body substance (*soma*). *Germens* are the germ cells from which descendants arise while the *soma* comprises all the rest of the body. Now the separation between the *germen* and the *soma* occurs in the first segmentations of the egg, in such a way that everything that happens to the body later—the characters which it acquires—remains without influence upon the *germen*, which transmits the hereditary patrimony directly from generation to generation.[32] Only through certain hereditary diseases can the *germen* be contaminated, but this would be only a source of degeneration, not of evolution.

This was the stone of offense over which the doctrine of Darwin stumbled, so that today it has been abandoned in its original form. Transformism then believed that it would be able to find its salvation in the theory of mutations. Hugo de Vries, the botanist, was actually able to declare, contrary to Darwin's conception of continuity, that nature makes sudden leaps. But this sudden appearance of new varieties which transmit their new characters to their descendants made it possible to imagine an evolution through natural selection. Unfortunately, however, these leaps occur only within the same species, never from one species to another. Manifestly, they constitute only a form of degeneration, a hereditary illness, and thus cannot explain a progressive linkage of the species.

The fourth salvo of objections comes from the finalists. The formation of an organ so complicated as the eye, they say, if it were to have been formed, as the Darwinists would have it, by a succession of fortuitous selections, would require such an extraordinary concourse of accidents that it would be literally inconceivable. A whole series of organs, such as the cornea, the vitreous humor, the retina, etc., each of which rendered no service whatsoever to the other, would have to have become what they are accidentally, simultaneously, and independently of one another. "Darwin himself used to say," writes L. Cuénot,[67] "that the problem of the formation of such a complex organ as the eye made him sick when he thought about it." And the eye is not an exceptional case, say the finalists. Nature abounds with ingenious inventions; organs of diverse origin appear to be so precisely calculated to complete each other that it is impossible to admit that they are the result of accident. Jean Rostand,[17] a champion of transformism, has described the "push buttons in the abdomen of the crab" and shown to what fathomless perplexity the study of them leads. He himself gives the answer to the argument of the long periods of time in nature to which one all too easily takes recourse: to appeal "to the thousands upon thousands of centuries," he writes, is "in a way to drown the mystery of time."

The only transformists who at least present us with an acceptable conception of the world are the finalistic transformists, that is to say, the spiritualists. Here, for example, is Lecomte du Noüy,[32] of the Pasteur Institute, who remains true to the idea of progressive evolution, but nevertheless declares that it is inconceivable unless one admits that there is a God who is directing it to the goal which he has chosen. This is to abandon accident, the fundamental element of Darwinism and its success in the last century, and to come back to a religious explanation of nature. Compare this with the appealing theory with which Dr. Tzanck also attempts to get out of the impasse, and which he himself summarizes as follows:

"1. Everything proceeds as if at the beginning of every adaptation there intervened a possibility of choice, a consciousness.

"2. Everything proceeds as if the acquisitions of consciousness were automatically repeated through matter in the form of memory.

"3. Once being is organized it is not only able to function independently of any intervention of the consciousness, but the existing organization also resists further adaptations."[23]

What nevertheless prevents finalistic transformism from being convincing is the fact that, though nature, as we have said, is rich in ingenious inventions, it is no less rich in absurdities and useless, detrimental complexities, which it is really difficult to ascribe to a God or a consciousness that directs evolution. "We observe both order and disorder," writes Bergson. "Why do the lizards have a pineal eye which does not see? . . . It must be acknowledged that everything is not coherent in nature."[68]

It is apparent that these judgments raise serious doubts about the theory of transformism. For a hundred years the scientists, who have been carried away by its seductive idea, have searched to discover something which would confirm it scientifically. But they continually encounter facts which suggest alternative interpretations. To put it mildly, the transformists are painfully embarrassed and they are frank to admit it. Why then does the doctrine continue to be taught as scientific truth in schools? Why does it appear without any restriction in all our textbooks? The answer to that question is given by one of the most authoritative scientists in this field, Professor P. Lemoine,[69] curator of the Paris Museum: "Evolution is a kind of dogma in which its priests no longer believe, but which they preserve for the people. One must have the courage to say this. . . ."

Understandably, this statement raised a row in scientific circles. It sounds almost like a joke for a scientist to utter the word "dogma," when, after all, it has been science which has been saying that it frees men from the servitude of dogmas. And yet, if there is no scientific proof for it, can we really give any other name to the evolutionism which is taught in our schools and which in turn undergirds and sanctifies the dogma of progress? And if it is preserved only for the people, is not this done in order to avoid having to confess that after three hundred years of research science finds itself confronted with a mystery which is more disquieting than those which preceded it?

We may add to Professor Lemoine's startling statement one by another paleontologist, Y. Delage:[70] "If there existed a scientific hypothesis other than that of the theory of descent to explain the origin of species, numerous transformists would abandon their present opinion as insufficiently proved." Elsewhere this scholar speaks even more clearly: "I here use the first person," he says, "in order to show that I am speaking in my own name and not that of the transformists, many of whom will be scandalized when they read this statement. Nevertheless, I am absolutely convinced that one is not a transformist for reasons drawn from natural history, but rather by reason of one's philosophical opinions."

This is confirmed by the most convinced transformists: "Our belief in evolution," writes Lecomte du Noüy,[32] "is at the moment still far more intuitive, or metaphysical, rather than scientific, in origin." "If the fact of evolution imposes itself upon us through the sum of our present knowledge," writes Caullery,[65] "the way in which it is accomplished is far from being elucidated." But it is precisely by this claim to be able to explain scientifically how it was accomplished that transformism proposes to prove evolution. Otherwise it remains a purely philosophical hypothesis. Listen again to Caullery: "There is no doubt that it was mechanistic ideas that led the scientists to extrapolate organized beings from simple one-celled beings and living matter from inert matter." Evolutionism "has the advantage of being a sort of natural prolongation of the mechanistic way of thinking." Thus it was mechanistic prejudice that contributed to the success of transformism, and on the other hand transformism was used to support the mechanistic conception of the world. But this is to beg the question, to assume what one should prove.

The reader should now recall what we said about the "repression of philosophy." If one rejects all philosophical explanation of the world, one simply ends with an unconscious philosophy. One is no longer conscious of the fact that the explanation of the world in which one believes and regards as scientific is in reality only a philosophical hypothesis. Darwin's doctrine was certainly a grandiose philosophical theory and men ought to examine it with care. But it was not a scientific truth and it does not explain all the facts.

We should not be too surprised to find some prejudices among men of science. In reality no one in this world is objective, the scientists no more than the masses. Everybody clings to certain ideas for emotional reasons, and everybody selects from the innumerable facts which he is able to observe those which confirm his ideas, and closes his eyes to those which contradict them. I do not claim to be more objective than all other men. I too gather together with unconcealed joy the works and the observations that corroborate my ideas. And since I have adopted certain views about healing, for example, my colleagues send me reports of clinical cases of cures which have followed upon a spiritual experience. A materialistic-minded doctor, on the other hand, promptly assumes that in such a case there has been an error in diagnosis. And he in turn emphasizes only those cases which conform with his philosophical ideas. But we have been told a lie when it has been asserted that belief in progress and evolution are the result of an objective examination of the facts.

What I say is therefore by no means a criticism of science. Everything it has given to us in the way of scientific knowledge is beyond discussion. The conscientiousness, the devotion with which generations of naturalists have observed and gathered facts, studied discoveries and experimentally established the connection of cause and effect are admirable. Their work will endure. The fossils they exhumed, the skulls they measured remain in our museums. It is these tangible realities to which we shall always have to return in order to understand nature a little better. But under the pretext of interpreting the facts the scientists often change their coats and in good faith and without fully realizing it become philosophers or prophets. They propagate theories which, one after another, must be abandoned again. But their ideas live on in the popular mind and possess a tenacious life. In the thinking of our contemporaries, to whom these ideas continue to be officially taught, a dogmatic statement of the doctrine of evolution remains one of the principal challenges to the Christian faith. How can we believe the Bible, they think, when the very first pages are refuted by science? Our first father was not Adam, not a perfect man created in the image of God, but a poor, primitive, unintelligent product of blind animal evolution, a link between the apes and us. All the discoveries of paleontology, they think, contradict the worldview which is given to us in Genesis.

Let us now look more closely into the problem of the origin of man. It constitutes, as we have seen, the stone of offense for the so-called "spiritualistic" transformism. In order to extricate himself from the difficulty, Dr. Trolliet[63] cites a certain Jean d'Estienne and the subtle exegetical distinction which he has introduced into the analysis of the creation story in Genesis. Where Genesis says "God created man" the word "created" is improper and really signifies "formed," that is to say, formed him through the means of evolution from the animal. The fragility of this argument is perhaps the best proof that in such arguments the transformists are obedient not to the imperatives of reason but rather to philosophical prejudices; and also the best proof that there is a mystical faith in progress that men do not want to abandon.

In reality one cannot adopt mechanistic transformism without denying the special creation of man, which is affirmed not only by one verse in Genesis but by the whole perspective of the Bible. Therefore, the transformists attach much importance to the animal origin of man. The principal paleontological discoveries which can be appealed to in this debate are: 1. In Lower Pleistocene, the jaw-bone of Maurer, the skull from Piltdown, the occiput of Swanscombe, and the femur from Java attributed to *Pithecanthropus*. 2. In Middle Pleistocene, the remains of Neanderthal man. 3. Finally, in Upper Pleistocene, the skeletons of Grimaldi and those of Cro-Magnon.

Everything went well as long as one found in the most recent strata only the fossils akin to present-day man and in the ancient strata skeletons more akin to the ape. But things began to go badly as soon as new discoveries brought to light in the ancient strata human remains which are more akin to present-day man than his alleged ancestors. Imagine the embarrassment of the transformists! Their whole theory of the origin of man collapses if skeletons of *Homo sapiens* are found in geological periods which lie farther back than *Pithecanthropus*. A number of scholars did not hesitate to dispute the authenticity of these discoveries. It was like being in the midst of a political fight! On the fossils of Castenedolo, G. Montandon[71] writes in a cool tone: "This *sapiens* would thus be older than any document human paleontology has produced up to this time; this is too extraordinary to be given any serious consideration today." We still recall the flutter into which the learned world was thrown by the discovery of the Swanscombe skull in June, 1935. "It is manifestly that of a *Homo sapiens*," allows G. Montandon, professor at the school of anthropology, "but the level at which it was discovered corresponds to the Lower Pleistocene, the Early Paleolithic. The importance of this concomitant circumstance led to the appointment of a commission of specialists to examine the site. But all of them with one accord declared that there could be no question of artificial shifting of the terrain; the skull had lain in its original place. . . . If the geologists are not mistaken, one is confronted with a *Homo sapiens* who is anterior to all the Neanderthal men." "If the geologists are not mistaken!" You see the point: the discovery is too important simply to be able to dispute it as was done with the preceding ones. So the insinuation is made that perhaps the geologists are off the track. But, assuming that they are off the track, then the whole argument of anthropology collapses, since it is based upon the dating of the various geological strata! And G. Montandon adds rather melancholically: "The discovery of Swanscombe and the consequent affirmation of the high value of Piltdown brought into prominence a number of earlier discoveries, the antiquity of which had been denied because of the morphology of the *sapiens* in the excavated skulls. However, according to certain authors, *sapiens* would go back to an even remoter past. Remains of him had been found in Tertiary and even Secondary terrane. A scholar as sober as M. Boule,[72] professor at the Paris Museum, impartially examines the motives which led Ales Hrdlicka to discard from the anthropological dossier all the fossils discovered in America. "Hrdlicka," he declares, "starts out with the principle that, in accord with the general development of the mammals, the fossil men must differ from present-day man." He goes on to say: "Such an assertion begs the question." In the same way in 1896 "a human fossil was discovered in Tertiary terrane (Lower Pliocene)" which was later disputed because it "was absolutely identical with that of a present-day Alsatian and consequently could not date from the Tertiary period."

We see how these men proceed: while the theory of evolution claims to be based upon scientific discoveries, it can serve on the contrary as a trick to eliminate these discoveries, that is, to retain those which are favorable to it and to reject those which are incompatible with it!

Other anthropologists are more cautious. In order to explain the presence of the Swanscombe skull in strata which are older than those of Neanderthal man, they launch into complicated hypotheses. They assume that there were a number of branches of humans, which detached themselves at various times from the simian trunk, the oldest of which goes farther back than all our paleontological documents. Here again we have the same procedure which we have already mentioned: an assumption which naturally can be formulated as one pleases, but which cannot be proved because it is lost in the night of time, in an epoch on which no discovery has yet cast any light.

The climax, however, is the story of the ape-man (*Pithecanthropus*). As is well known, in the year 1890 a young Dutch surgeon, Eugene Dubois, enthused by reading Ernest Haeckel's

transformist theory, journeyed to Java to search for fossils which
would confirm it. He had very good luck, for before the year
was out he triumphantly announced to the enthusiastic learned
world the discovery of the top of a skull and several teeth be-
longing to an ape, and, fifteen meters away, the femur of a man.
He needed nothing more than this to assume that all of these
remains belonged to one and the same person, who was then
baptized with the pompous name *Pithecanthropus erectus.* At
the World Exposition of 1900 the crowds were able to admire a
reconstruction of this famous ancestor and extol the progress of
science. Everybody could compare himself to him to his own
advantage!

Unfortunately, Dr. Dubois had announced the finding of three
teeth, but had described only two of them. The third was not
described until 1930 and was not modeled until 1937. About
this, however, Professor Montandon[71] says, "All the scholars
agreed unanimously that it was a human tooth." Why then had
Dr. Dubois failed to describe it, just as he had neglected to
describe two skulls of *Homo sapiens* which he had found in
Java the year before? Quite simply, says Montandon, because
it "is very certain that if Dubois had announced in 1894 the discovery of two simian teeth and one human tooth, the idea would
certainly have prevailed that all of these bones did not belong
to the same individual, and this was done for the sake of *Pithecanthropus.* In the terrane explored by Dr. Dubois there were,
quite simply, remains of apes and remains of humans. And poor
Pithecanthropus, today abandoned by the scientists, has flown
away into the land of legend where he has joined the Minotaur.
But he lives on in the mind of masses, who continue to believe
that science has proved the animal origin of man. If one found
in excavations a human femur and the skull of a bull, say Salet
and Lafont[58] (to whom I owe these details), one could equally
assert that the Minotaur really and truly existed.

Under the title "Regressive Evolution,"[58] Salet and Lafont present a new theory of evolution. The theory they offer sounds strange—even outlandish—to many modern ears, heretofore filled with the Darwinian doctrine. Although their views remain to be proved or disproved, in the same way as the transformist views, it is useful to open one's mind to their suggestive interpretation, if only to realize that other alternatives to Darwin are possible. But it is somewhat closer to the picture presented in the Bible. One is not surprised that, like everything new, it is meeting with a very reserved reception on the part of the scientists. The foreword to the book, however, is written by one of the most thorough geologists of our time, Professor Raguin. "Already," he writes, "the system bears the stamp of harmony and grandeur. It radiates an undeniable force and convincingness and it merits our passionate support."

After a criticism of transformism (from which I have made large borrowings in the preceding pages), the authors develop their hypothesis in the form of an apologue: Imagine, they say, that a mechanic today, in order to set in motion a water pump, attached to it an ancient automobile. Imagine further that after many, many centuries excavations brought to light this hybrid machine. The finalists would then cry out: Such a machine cannot be the result of accident; only a creative mind could have invented it. Look how the valves, the pistons, and the carburetor work together! All of this is manifestly organized to work together. But their opponents, the mechanists, would marshal their grave objections: If a mind really directed this construction, why did he put a speedometer in a stationary machine? Why did he furnish it with headlights which do not even illuminate the pump? And the Bergsonians would also put in an appearance and try to reconcile the conflicting views: There is an *élan vital*, a vital energy, which is sometimes blind and sometimes clear-sighted. It produces some remarkable things and also some absurd things. That's just what *élan vital* is.

The true explanation would finally be given by somebody who posed the following question: Why not assume that this machine was originally very well adapted to its purpose, that it was later utilized for another use, namely, to drive a water pump, so that the apparent absurdity is explained by this misuse of it?

In the same way, confronted by the contradictory arguments of the finalists, the mechanists, and the Bergsonians, Salet and Lafont begin with the assumption that "present-day beings sprang, by a process of regressive evolution, from living beings which in the past were in their way as perfect as it is possible for creatures to be." We see that here we are again approaching the biblical view. The golden age lies behind us. The world created by God was perfect. All of the great zoölogical groups, between which no transitional forms have ever been discovered, were created in the beginning. Likewise man, whose remains are being found in ever more ancient strata, was created in the beginning and in a perfect state. Since nothing in nature explains death, there is nothing to oppose the idea that this man did not die so long as there was nothing that disturbed the perfect harmony of this perfect world. But we can also understand why even the slightest disobedience to such a harmony led to a gradual disorder, not only in man, whose fault it was, but also in the whole of nature, bringing with it deforestation, the changing seasons, the catastrophe of the carboniferous period, and so on. In this disordered world, living beings were confronted by new conditions of life and "evolution was the adaptation to a disordered world." In every species it represents a certain degeneration of the perfect primitive types. With regard to the Neanderthal man, for example, Salet and Lafont make this comment: "It is evident that these fossils can just as well have descended by a process of regression from men who were like the man of today as from the primates compared with which they represent a progression." Thus it is not the animal which progressively became man, but rather certain human races . . . retrograded to animality."

But if no vestiges of original man can now be found, the

question may be asked: Why are there no traces of his culture? Salet and Lafont reply that our whole culture is the result of the disturbed state which menaces man. In a perfect nature he had no need to protect himself against cold and hunger.

I shall not relate here all the details of the theory. I refer the reader to the work itself. And I also recall to his mind what I said at the beginning of this chapter, namely, that all these things should not be taken as final—or even too seriously. We should learn to laugh a bit over the successive theories which men fabricate in order to explain the world and which they are so prone to believe are definitive. At all events it can be said that the Salet-Lafont theory fits much of the present scientific data as well as the classical theory of evolution.

I am not here taking a position. But if at first the views of Salet and Lafont cause us to smile, may it not be because we are all saturated with the Darwinian theory, even though one of its most authoritative adherents has told us that he would be glad to abandon it if there were another plausible explanation?

What if the biblical account is closer to the truth? What if the Genesis account, far from being simply an assortment of myths, presents a realistic picture? Up to this time not a single proof to the contrary has been produced. What then? Why, then this would mean that men have rejected the biblical explanation of the world for emotional reasons. Like the adolescent of whom we spoke, they have merely fabricated new theories in the spirit of contradiction to their forefathers, and stubbornly cling to them despite other arguments in order not to be proved wrong. In any case, let us acknowledge that the world of nature, with its strange mélange of marvels and absurdities, ingenious discoveries and mysterious anomalies, is far better explained by the hypothesis of a perversion of the original harmony than by the idea of blind and uninterrupted progress.

The influence of Darwinian doctrine upon our modern world

appears to me to be immense. It goes considerably beyond the compass of natural history. The fact that our contemporaries firmly believe an inadequately documented theory of animal evolution is in itself a misfortune. But in addition, with this theory they have been inculcated, as has already been shown, with a faith in a new trinity: accident, struggle, and progress. And this trinity is one of the idols of the modern world; it determines the destiny of society and the individual. We do not realize this because modern specialization has put walls of partition between the various disciplines, so that sociologists see only the sociological factors in the unrolling of history, the economists only the economic factors, and the psychologists only the psychological factors. But life does not recognize the walls of partition, and a theory of nature which everyone learns in school exercises its influence upon the behavior and the thinking of all men.

After all, it is clear that if all our children are taught that the animal kingdom created itself progressively in the course of the centuries, without the intervention of any other God except accident and the struggle for existence, then to the whole world these three fundamental notions of accident, struggle, and progress must come to be accepted as the great laws of life.

Accident: Every epoch implicitly teaches a philosophy, without rendering any further account of it, since it is completely undisputed. Accident is the first article in the creed of this unconscious philosophy of our time. Faith in chance has robbed modern man of his sense of moral responsibility. When he falls ill, he blames it on chance: accident has brought him in contact with noxious microbes. He does not ask himself why his neighbor, who was also exposed to them, was not infected. If he has a quarrel with his wife, he complains of his "bad luck" in getting tied up with a nervous woman who is impossible to live with. In every situation this exempts him from having to look for the responsibility for his destiny within himself. This is why our world is full of complaints, recriminations, and demands.

And all this engenders bitterness, envy, desire for revenge, and strife, so that the chaos is increased and along with it the curses against fate. It is clear that society cannot organize itself harmoniously in this concourse of irritations.

If everything is accidental, then the only rule of life is to let all considerations go and seize opportunity by the forelock. If happiness is no longer the blessing promised to those who obey the laws of God, but only a blind stroke of fate, then the greatest possible shrewdness is the best rule of life. And when everyone wants to be the shrewdest, existence finally becomes nothing more than intrigue, lies, and dodges. And the conflicts and injustices that result, far from causing men to examine themselves and become honest again, only drive them to resort even more to these poisonous weapons in order to conjure away their bad luck: they certainly are not going to be left holding the bag.

Struggle: Even more serious is the fact that the world took from Darwin the belief that progress results automatically from the universal struggle in which the strong are victorious over the weak, the more cunning over those who are more honest. It is well known that the fundamental idea of the Darwinian theory is precisely the idea that the struggle for existence is the great law of nature and the source of progress.

Today there is hardly anybody who does not believe this. And yet nothing is easier than to find examples in nature that contradict it. In the age of the enormous dinosaurs, whose mighty skeletons can be admired in the museums, the mammals vegetated in minuscule forms, so small, writes Lecomte du Noüy,[32] that the gigantic reptiles in one step crushed hundreds of them without even noticing it." Now the dinosaurs have disappeared —just as many of our gigantic modern institutions will undoubtedly vanish—*because they were too large*. Just as that unhappy animal, the machaerodont (saber-toothed tiger), whose teeth became so mighty that it could no longer close its mouth when feeding, disappeared. And the poor little mammals of the dinosaur age have become the royal branch of creation.

In reality nature is neutral. But we view the spectacle it presents to us through the colored glasses of our own philosophy. This is why we always find in it the confirmation of our view of the world. Hitherto nature has been described for us as the arena of a universal struggle in which the strong are always victorious. But it could just as well be described as a universal community in which the humblest are just as useful as the strongest and each one can survive only as he fulfills the role, the vocation to which he has been called in this great harmony. What would happen to the animals, which are incapable of fixing nitrogen, without the plants which furnish it for them?

You can with Darwin profess a philosophy of progress through struggle, but you do not have the right to assert that it is based upon the scientific observation of nature. But this is precisely the question! For our contemporaries believe that it accords with the implacable laws of nature. They think that only the man who shows his teeth, who gives blow for blow or even strikes first contributes to the progress of the world. We know that these views are openly avowed by the military, who are among those chiefly responsible for the catastrophes which have smitten mankind. They maintain that war is necessary for the progress of humanity because in war a selection of the stronger is effected.

But he who denounces these men is not always aware of how deeply he himself is contaminated with this idea.

The whole doctrine of liberalism is based upon Darwin's idea. It assumes that the economic progress of society will result from a ruthless competitive struggle in industry and commerce. It represents this struggle as a law of nature, as the source of "natural selection." It believes this so firmly that it is absolutely blind to the inextricable difficulties brought about by liberal economy and of which the mighty victors are the victims just as much as the martyrs whom they have immolated on the altar of competition and struggle.

But Marxism, which opposes liberalism, actually professes the same fundamental philosophy. For the competitive struggle it has substituted the class struggle, but again it is the struggle from which progress is expected. And it too believes so firmly in this struggle that it is blind to the misery it brings to humanity, which it says it wants to save.

Modern parliamentarianism rests upon the peculiar idea that progress is the result of a perpetual battle between the parties, that right and justice emerge from the struggle between accusation and defense, and that truth arises from the clash of two assertions, neither of which is in search of the truth.

Whether it be our families or our domestic or foreign policy, this philosophy of struggle has poisoned everything. Everybody thinks he must defend himself at any cost and give his neighbor as many whacks as possible in order not to be trampled upon. Everybody moans about the whacks he gets, but while only a very few look for the fault within themselves they all denounce the faults of their adversaries. However, in this case at least, their indictment is not based upon the ideal of struggle, but rather upon the Christian ideal of justice, fairness, honesty, fellowship, and love, which despite everything they have never altogether lost.

Finally, *progress:* When we stop to think seriously about this, it seems inconceivable that progress should result from this jumble of unfettered accidents, struggles, and injustices. Nevertheless, an unquestioned evolutionism has succeeded in making the whole world believe this. Darwin's theory inoculated the human mind with a robust optimism which resists all the contradictions of history.

The Bible portrays man as the masterpiece of God and his unhappiness as the consequence of the misuse of this masterpiece. Transformism, on the contrary, portrays him as the glorious culmination of a blind evolution which automatically produces itself through the prolongation of struggle. There is no doubt that man is not perfect; but the fact that he is not *more* perfect than he is, is not because of his sin, but rather because he is *not yet* perfect; and this he will become through the unlimited progress of history. A very flattering view, as we see. This prospect has given the modern world an incredible confidence in man. He no longer needs to examine himself. He will accomplish his salvation by constantly marching forward, from progress to progress, through the development of his knowledge, his discoveries, his science. How far will he be able to go? "There is nothing that is unknowable," cries Professor Gustave Roussy,[73] rector of the University of Paris, "even though we foresee that we shall never fathom the depths of the abyss, even though it is wise, even though it is prudent to admit that we shall never exhaust the inexhaustible unknown."

I need not emphasize the relationship of this confidence in man to Darwin's thinking, to the whole thought of Nietzsche, of which we will speak later, and how much it has influenced the myth of Nazism; but it also betrays itself in the mystical faith in technology which is common to the two great powers of today, the United States and Russia.

What is paradoxical is the fact that this great confidence in man has dehumanized our civilization. "In spite of the political and social theories which appear to exalt man," writes Dr. Menkès,[40] "human personality has never been so disregarded."

Since the doctrine of transformism is essentially mechanistic, progress is expected to come from an impersonal mechanism, not from man himself. From the technical development of law it is expected that peace will come; from technological improvement will come a new art; from a more advanced science of economics will come prosperity.

This myth of progress, resulting from an ever increasing network of codes and regulations, which claim to anticipate and provide for everything, is the basis of the administrative degeneration of our modern world. We need only to look at the incredible degree of bureaucracy which has now been attained in a country as advanced as America to guess what to expect tomorrow.

And life? "Progress," writes Dr. de Rougemont,[11] "has certainly made our life much more agreeable, but I do not think that it has promoted life."

One must be blinded by prejudice not to see that progress is a myth. A beautiful myth, if you please, a beautiful dream which has stirred great devotion. But a myth of human invention. We have been made to believe that it has been drawn from nature. But nature offers us as many examples of degeneration as of progress. A pure picture of progress in nature, happening in a completely mechanical way, is an affirmation of pseudo-scientific faith, not a conclusion of genuinely scientific knowledge.

Nor does progress appear in history. All the discoveries, all the conquests, all the institutions of humanity do not alter its true problem. Why was Dr. Alexis Carrel's book, *Man, the Unknown,* so successful? Was it not because man instinctively felt that he was better understood by this great scholar, who called him the unknown, than by all the little scholars who claimed to know him? Was it not because man instinctively felt that there is something true in this voice which denounces the vanity of a prodigious technical progress in medicine which leaves him alone with his interior illness, from which he suffers the most?

This is not a question of denigrating science or technology. Man thirsts for truth. The joy of the scholar who discovers a particle of the truth is a legitimate joy. The joy of the technician who solves a technical difficulty is a legitimate joy. In my consulting room I have occasionally experienced the joy of having a part of the incomparable spectacle of a life which is changed, of a soul meeting his God and saying Yes to Him. But in my workshop I also know the joy of constructing an ingenious electric mechanism. There is room in my heart for these two kinds of joy which are not incompatible.

But the philosophy of progress robs man of the true joys, and the others become delusive. When scientific research and technical invention become a vain pursuit of progress instead of a joyous adventure they enslave men and assume oppressive proportions. "Behind all the convulsions in the political, economic, social, and cultural spheres there is the crisis of man himself," writes Dr. Maeder.[2] "Failing to recognize his limitations, man went beyond them and became titanic. Our age is a Promethean age."

We are familiar with Bergson's comment: "Humanity groans, half crushed under the burden of the progress it has made." And even Balzac wrote: "Progress is nonsense."

Nevertheless, I will finally be asked: Is it not dangerous to take away from man this hope of a better future? Will he not sink into pessimism? Well, if I begin to promise a cure to a sick person whom I have given up as lost in order to revive his morale, the comfort I would bring to him would be of very short duration. The constant progress of his illness would soon shatter his confidence and with the approach of death the longer I had deceived him the more helpless he would find himself. Do we not find among people today indications of the same disillusionment in the face of events which have tragically belied the fine optimism of the beginning of the century? They are in danger of suddenly falling into complete skepticism. "Whenever a man chooses," writes Sartre,[3] "whatever may be his purpose . . . it is impossible for him to prefer another; . . . we do not believe in progress."

Our Christian faith has no more to do with this naïve confidence in the progress of man than with the cynical despair of Sartre. "Would it not be easier to hope for a better life," ask Salet and Lafont,[58] "if one could attain to the certainty that the world, when it came from the hands of the Creator, was 'good'? For if in the beginning, as we have been told, God created only an imperfect world, how is it possible to conceive that a blind mechanism, automatic and inherent in this imperfect world, could ever bring it to ultimate perfection? On the other hand, if God was able to create a perfect world, has he not the power to restore it to its original perfection? This is the Christian hope, not only the hope of the upsurge of the human soul liberated from nature, but rather of the resurrection and redemption of the whole of nature. 'For,' writes St. Paul, 'the creation was subjected to futility, not of its own will but by the will of him who subjected it in hope; because the creation itself will be set free from its bondage to decay and obtain the glorious liberty of the children of God. We know that the whole creation has been groaning in travail together until now; and not only the creation, but we ourselves . . . as we wait for adoption as sons, the redemption of our bodies.' "74

CHAPTER V

The Myth of Power

THE THEORY OF the world which Darwin bequeathed to us is thus more a fiction than a work of science. Nevertheless it forms our contemporary thinking. It not only inculcates in us the idea of progress, but also gives us a dynamic ideal, as is manifested by the unusual currency of this term today. We have been told that here below everything is struggle—the blind struggle of one species against the other, the struggle of individuals within the species, the struggle for existence, the struggle of competition, the universal triumph of the stronger over the weaker. Perhaps it is a small comfort to think that progress will result from this universal battle; but more than anything else this intimates to us that the most important thing in this world is to be strong. This idea deserves to be examined separately, because of the very considerable influence which it has exercised upon the development of our society. Progress as such is still a relatively disinterested and abstract goal. But when we reflect upon it more deeply it turns out to be only a rationalization by which man justifies his instinctive behavior and his egotism; for if he seeks to be or to appear to be strong, the implication is that he is doing this rather and quite simply for fear of being trampled in life.

This ideal of power is common to all contemporary movements, it contaminates everything, even the Christian church. Whether we are partisans or adversaries of the class struggle, we all practice it. Whether we are nationalists or internationalists, we engage in war. Whether we believe in a one-party system or competing parties, we all practice power politics. Whether we are for a free economy or a planned economy, we are all looking for economic power.

Salvation lies in power.

I prepared this book in the same region where Nietzsche conceived his doctrine of Superman and the will to power. "In those days at Lake Silvaplana," he wrote, "I walked through the forest; at a mighty pyramid-shaped rock not far from Surlei I stopped. There this thought came to me."[1] In me, however, the high mountain stirred the feeling of the smallness of man and the greatness of God; one more proof of the fact that each one of us sees in nature the image that conforms to his own tendency of mind.

The influence of Nietzsche is immense. I recently met a friend of mine, the chaplain of a large organization of young Catholic workers. "It is unbelievable," he said, "how the thinking of Nietzsche has penetrated everywhere, how many of our young people almost literally quote this thinker, without having read him, indeed, without even knowing him."

His teaching is well known. Morality, he says, is the sin against the spirit of the earth. It is an invention of the weak, who make a virtue of their weakness. Since they cannot endure either the sight of the real world or the force of those individuals who are on the way toward the Superman, they have canonized everything that is inferior and promulgate as the highest virtue that which to the strong is the greatest vice, namely, pity.

It is not surprising that adolescents are enthusiastic over Nietzsche. This is the occasion to emphasize once more the relationship between the modern mentality and that of an adolescent in the midst of the crisis of development, who denounces the moral principles by which he has been reared, saying that up to now they have stifled his spirit and prevented him from realizing himself, from living his life and developing and manifesting his power.

But above all I should like to show here that this doctrine

is by no means limited to the circle of Nietzsche's adherents, but that it pervades all of us more or less. "Nietzsche is an inclination, an inclination in every one of us," writes Henri Maldiney.[1] Which of us can boast that he has escaped this modern view that regards pity, forgiveness, compassion, love as a weakness? Max Picard[75] has shown in his book *L'homme du néant,* the German title of which, *Hitler in uns* ["The Hitler in Us"], is more suggestive, that it is not enough to fight against German Nazism, that rather it is important to recognize that it could not have flourished if the whole world had not already accepted a criterion of power from which it is very hard to detach ourselves. Picard maintains that this modern world no longer had any directing spiritual principle, that it had substituted dynamic action for the ideas of order, harmony, and truth, and was ready to admire every manifestation of power.

To be sure, there has always been and always will be in man a temptation to exert his own power and to destroy that of others. The fable of the wolf and the lamb was not invented today. Nevertheless, what characterizes the modern world is that it has elevated this inclination into a law of nature. Formerly when men yielded to it they still did not deny the immorality of what they did. But today they justify it by measuring the value of man by his action and the power of his action.

"The philosophers have hitherto done nothing but interpret the world in different ways. Now it must be transformed," declared the manifesto of Marxism. According to René Gillouin,[19] there is more in this than only a Marxist concept. It is really a question of our concept of man as such. For the man who creates (*Homo faber*) and the knowing man who followed him (*Homo sapiens*), the modern world has substituted the man who acts (*Homo agens*). The nobility of man then resides neither in what he creates nor in what he thinks, but in the power of his external action. "Man is nothing but that which he makes of himself," says Sartre.[3] And if man makes or thinks something, this has virtue only insofar as it is great. All of us moderns have written this criterion of the power and greatness of man deep down in our hearts. When the first trolley bus line was recently put in service in the city where I live, Genevans read with pride in the newspaper that these vehicles were the biggest, the heaviest, and the most efficient in all Switzerland. Nobody bothered to ask whether the highway was firm enough to support them. And so it is in all areas. Everything must always be growing bigger, the commercial buildings, the factories, the trusts, the apartment houses, and the hotels.

You may say to me that back in the Middle Ages the cathedrals were already very large in comparison with the small houses that squatted around them. True, but in the minds of their builders the value of these cathedrals lay not in their size but rather in the harmony of their proportions. The idea of inner harmony has since been replaced by the idea of achieving records. This development goes hand in hand with the repression of the spiritual of which we spoke above: it is the negation of value in itself.

Let us recall the four storeys of man which we described (see p. 50), following Dr. de Rougemont,[11] and his definition of health, namely, the proper precedence of personhood. In direct opposition to this ideal, modern man, in order to gain power, seeks to develop to the maximum that one of the four storeys in which he excels. If he has muscles, he goes after record performances in sport; if he possesses imagination, he seeks to dominate others through his power of suggestion; if he has intellectual ability, he concentrates solely upon this; if he has spiritual experience, he specializes in this and disregards concrete realities.

In this race for power the modern world finds nothing but disharmony. What kind of people are honored today? The sports heroes, the demagogues, the rich, the scientists. Not the all-round man, not the humanist of the Renaissance, but rather the man who has developed to the point of hypertrophy the trumps he plays in life.

Speaking of the "ideal of militant Communists," Pierre Hervé[1] mentions as its "ultimate important quality: the concern for efficiency." But of course this word "efficiency" is on everybody's lips, not only those of Communists. The whole of life is viewed from the angle of tactics and strategy. The value of an idea lies in its efficiency, its effectiveness. The criterion of truth is success. Even Christian apologetics is infected with it; it sometimes attempts to prove the power of Christianity by demonstrating its effectiveness, by the victories which it assures in life. This is a theology of success and not a theology of the Cross. All this is related to our Darwinian conception of nature, according to which the strong will always devour the weak and the truth will be destroyed if we are not strong enough to defend it. The elephant is much stronger than the lamb; nevertheless it does not devour it, because its instinct, its inner law, does not impel him to do so. True, there are in nature the strong who devour the weak, but there are also the weak who devour the strong. The law of the strongest is not universal. But what is universal is the law of harmony which bestows upon each being in nature its own destiny and its function within the whole.

By trying to justify the law of the strongest in the name of nature we today have undermined the whole concept of harmony, of sacrifice, of order, and finally of community. I see many married people in conflict. And I think that my colleagues will agree with me when I confess here how difficult it is to compose these conflicts. If a true spiritual revolution does not take place in the couple, our efforts will be in vain. For what stands in their way is this very idea—so widespread today—that one must be strong in order not to be pushed to the wall and that to give in is a proof of weakness. That there is true greatness in making concessions, that forgiveness is a real victory, and that to renounce one's own will is a true joy—these are ideas which have almost disappeared today. It is obvious that in such

an atmosphere no real community is possible. Each of the partners constantly talks about having to "defend his personality,"
and all the while his personality is being completely consumed
and deformed by this strife. If one party manifests a certain
inclination or taste, the other cannot go along for fear that it
will look as if he is being taken in tow. And the other party
clings fast to his view for fear of losing his originality.

It is precisely this obsessive fear of being pushed to the wall
that gave rise to the modern emancipation of woman. It caused
her to lose her femininity by forcing her always to measure herself in everything by the man. We have been led to believe that
the relationship of persons is only a relationship of force and
this delusion has falsified our whole society.

It may be objected that Marxism by proclaiming the ideal of
equality is actually aiming to put an end to this destruction of
the weak by the strong. But there are bourgeois people who
attribute to the Marxists an egalitarianism which they themselves
deny. "Egalitarianism has no place in Marxist thinking," writes
Pierre Hervé.[1] "Marxism has never been based upon equality.
If it desires to create an equality, it is the equality of opportunity, the equality of starting from the same place, the equality
for developing the legitimate and inevitable inequalities. If
it desires to suppress certain inequalities, they are those inequalities which capitalistic society has introduced into the free play
of vocations and legitimate ambitions." Very well, let us con-
cede that the bourgeois attribute to the Marxists an egalitarianism which they themselves do not profess. They do this in order
to refute their opponent by appealing to the example of nature,
where everything is allegedly nothing but unjust inequality and
destruction of the weak by the strong, which at the same time
excuses the injustices committed by the capitalist regime. The
inequalities of nature, however, are more qualitative than quantitative; they are less a relationship of forces than a diversity of
functions. In reality both the capitalistic and the Marxist views
present us with a view of life which is a destructive struggle of

the strong against the weak and not a harmonious cooperation of complementary values.

Life is a battle. From childhood this slogan is presented to us and inculcated in us. And what is more, we are not told that this slogan means the battle against ourselves but simply against others. This begins at school where individualism is cultivated with a vengeance, where in every subject students are constantly compelled to measure their "strength" by that of their comrades, where they are censured if they help a fellow student, because this upsets the relationship of forces. The ideal that is impressed upon the mind of the student is constantly to show that one is stronger than the other and not the ideal of helping the weak to become stronger. And all too often, as Dr. Allendy[5] has shown, the teacher himself suggests that the weak are to be scorned and gives the sign for their persecution by the rest of the class. "You will never amount to anything in life if you do not do better work." To begin with, this phrase, repeated in a thousand different ways, is false; for we know very well that it is not always the best students whose life later on is the most productive. Furthermore, it does not stimulate the child to work, but rather paralyzes him by causing him to despair of himself. It can actually produce psychological catastrophes. And finally, it represents work not as a service for others but as an armor which the child must put on in order not to be crushed by life.

In this regimen of perpetual competition, this obsession with marks and rankings, the weak constantly grow weaker and the strong stronger. For the weak lose their courage because they are inhibited by inferiority feelings which are suggested to them. And the strong, stimulated by the flattering praise of their teachers, dream only of triumph over their competitors and imagine that their value in life will be measured by their victories over others. Thus the school launches two kinds of people upon society: the "crushed" and the "crushers," both of which constitute a danger to the harmonious play of forces in society.

I have mentioned Dr. Allendy. Read his fine book *L'enfance*

méconnue[5] ["Neglected Childhood"] and you will get an impressive picture of this tragedy of childhood through which all
men must pass. It is the school of jealousy in which the child,
at home as well as in the classroom, learns constantly to compare himself with others, to despise the weaker, to envy the
stronger, and to regard his equals as enemies, in which he feels
that his emotional reactions are not understood and that he
is not appreciated for his human value but solely for what he
is able to accomplish.

But what solution does Dr. Allendy offer? Secular psychology
is still dominated by the myth of power. Why are psychological
institutes continuing to multiply? And why do people today attend them in such numbers? They go to find out how to become
"strong," how to become strong in this universal struggle for
existence. And yet the strength which psychology gives us
leaves us weak in the face of the real problems of life. Dr.
Allendy's widow possessed the tragic honesty to publish his
Journal d'un médecin malade[76] ["Diary of a Sick Physician"],
which he kept to the last day of his long agony of dying. Nothing could show us more poignantly the futility of a life that
possesses everything except faith. This generous-hearted man,
this marvelous intelligence, this fine psychologist, who penetrated so deeply into the human soul, possessed nothing in the
face of death but the most hopeless kind of cynicism. Once
more we observe how adversaries coincide in a common error:
the school that disregards the laws of psychology and the psychologist who seeks in them only a means to success, both are
trying to persuade modern man that the essential thing in life
is to be strong.

This is why we find in all the patients who come to consult
us a more or less conscious false shame of their illness, which
only aggravates their situation. The sensitive are ashamed of
their sensitiveness; they regard it not as a gift but rather as a
weakness which they must try to repress, and this only makes
them worse. The mentally ill, even those who admit that they

rather enjoy their illness as a welcome refuge, are ashamed of their condition. They neglect themselves in order to give the impression that they are not overly concerned with themselves. They have a constant need to justify themselves in the face of the scorn which they feel the strong have for them. This falsifies their reactions and merely complicates their mental difficulties.

However, if this modern criterion of power has a devastating effect upon the weak, it is no less dangerous for the strong, even though it is less apparent. Here again we must quote Dr. Baruk,[13] who has so incisively shown that whoever benefits by an injustice suffers from a bad conscience. True, he soon represses his pangs, but this warps his whole behavior and provokes social catastrophes. "Bring several people together," he writes, "and the first conflict will arise from wounded self-love, from the jealousy of one over against the other, sometimes from the feeling of inferiority, sometimes—and above all—from the feeling of guilt. . . . Then the reactions of defense and justification begin to operate: the attempt is made to shift the discontent upon innocent victims, to ward off criticism and justified complaints by creating artificial culprits. The weakest are well designed to play this role of the scapegoat. . . . The most atrocious civil wars, the crimes of fanaticism, and the wars of religion, or the ideological wars, are first fomented by agitators, by the enterpreneurs of hate, and only then do the base instincts of the masses explode."

Thus modern man, spurred by the spirit of our times to repress the voice of his conscience, hides his weaknesses behind his aggressive attitude. He covers up the struggle within himself and projects it outwardly in a battle with others. He is like the young man, whose case is reported by Dr. Maeder, who rises up against his father, his principal, society, plays the strong man, pours out indictments, and acts aggressively. But down inside he is troubled. He has, if I may put it this way, an unconscious consciousness of his weakness. He hides it from himself, precisely because he has been persuaded of an ideal of power which is literally inhuman. Then he is afraid of himself and afraid that others will discover his weakness. The strong of this world are the weak who are hiding their weakness. The righteous in this world are the sinners who denounce the faults of others to justify themselves. And they have to go on preaching the modern doctrine of power in order to shore up this tottering edifice of a society which admires those who look strong and scorns those who look weak.

A friend of mine, a scout leader, told me recently that the father of one of his boys came to see him one evening. "I want to explain to you," he said, "why I have taken my son away from your troop. It is because he is taking the scout law too seriously. He is too naïve. You know that all scouts repeat the words 'A scout is honest,' and yet they all know that it is impossible to put this into practice in life. But my son takes this seriously and in life he will be pushed to the wall."

This fear that their child may be crushed in life if he does not play the skin game of society is the more or less conscious anxiety of many parents. Here again we meet the conflict of which I have spoken. Such parents preach honesty to their child. But he senses very clearly that they fear he will suffer grievous consequences if he adheres to their preachments. And all over the world the fear of being crushed prevents people from being honest, bringing social disorder in its train, and this social disorder multiplies the catastrophes and thus again the fear of being crushed. It is fear that provokes war and war aggravates the fear. And the more the world allows itself to be sucked into this vortex the more each one struggles for power, power at any price, until the thermonuclear bomb or some still mightier weapon to come will crush the whole world.

I want to avoid any misunderstanding here. It is simply a fact that evil is powerful in the world. But then the strong must resist it, not so much to protect themselves as to protect the weak and to safeguard justice. Where would we be today if generous powers had not been willing to overthrow the Nazi power, which arose directly from this myth of power? I belong to a little country, which, next to God's protection, benefits from the protection of international order and the sacrifices which the strong consent to make in order to safeguard it. It is only proper that I should acknowledge what my country owes to them. Pascal has shown us that if justice has no power, then force will replace justice. But this is not the root of the myth of power. It consists rather in believing in the virtue of power itself. It is catastrophe when evil triumphs, but it is an even greater catastrophe if it compels the just to resort to injustice in order to combat it. Unless the world returns to moral conscience, to the value of the spirit and to its primacy over force, power is only a source of destruction.

Also connected with the myth of power is the modern world's distortion of the intellect. Part of the reason why the state supports public education is that it thereby gains power. When men strive by means of science to plumb the secrets of nature they do so partly in order to capture its forces. And again this would be perfectly legitimate if it were not at the same time proclaimed that science is morally neutral and asserted that it has no concern with the use which is made of the new forces it gives to men.

"It was probably a presumptuous error," wrote André George,[1] the physicist, after the event of Bikini, "to confuse the progress of science with the progress of humanity." And he quotes Louis de Broglie, who confesses that "he would not declare without reservations, as he would have several years ago, that 'one must love science because it is a great work of the spirit.'"

As far as the individual is concerned, on the other hand, it is mainly in order to be stronger in the battle of life, and not so much because of a thirst for knowledge, that modern people study more. If many parents keep their sons, and more recently their daughters, at their studies, it is not always because they

have a desire for a university career. It is often simply in order
to give them that trump card in life which is represented by a
bachelor's or a master's or a doctor's degree. Their children
will have a better chance of obtaining a position—even in industry and business—if they have a diploma from high school
or college. This tendency completely falsifies our concept of
intellectual culture and is a grave menace to the university. Instead of being what it was formerly, the hearth of disinterested
culture, it becomes an instrument in the pursuit of power. And
this sustains the great illusion that extension of knowledge is
the same thing as the intellectual progress of humanity. "No
matter how greatly the treasury of knowledge has been en-
riched," writes Charles Baudouin,[77] "intellectual capacities have
not increased during the course of history."

From science, technology was born, and its present vogue
likewise has its source in the myth of power. Combined in it
are the power of knowledge and the power of money. Technology, the fruit of knowledge, procures economic power. This
gives it its primacy in the modern world. "The only categorical
imperative which is still effective and universally obeyed," writes
René Gillouin,[52] "is the technico-scientific commandment: Thou
shalt invent, thou shalt apply, thou shalt above all things create
power, without concerning thyself in the least with the use
which will be made of it. . . . As if power were the supreme
value."

The more I seek to study men in the daily encounters of my
life the more clear it becomes to me that there are only a few
who seek money for its own sake or for the pleasure it provides.
It is much more the power that it bestows which constitutes the
deep motivation of the hot pursuit of money in our day. Unfortunately, we must recognize that whoever possesses, if not money,
then at least credit or the reputation of being rich, has possibilities not only of existing but also of performing useful service for
society which others do not have. The physician to whom the
poor confide is shocked to see the incredible injustice of our

modern society. Certainly it is neither the personal value of man
nor his talents which count today. And this is precisely the result
of that repression of the spiritual which is the peculiar malady
of the modern world. And this illness—we have seen its relation
to war and now we see it in connection with money—provokes
reactions which aggravate the evil. Fear of being trampled down
by society provokes the scramble for profits and this scramble for
profits falsifies and warps our economic life, deranges it, creates
insecurity, and there you have the vicious circle.

This is what has distorted the concept of work in our day.
Work has value in itself, insofar as it is service, and it does not
derive its value from the wealth it procures. On the basis of my
medical practice, I can make a very grave statement, whose immense economic consequences anyone can estimate: the great
majority of the people who come to me do not like their work;
they look upon it only as a way of making a living. "It is possible
to achieve distinction," writes Theo Spoerri,[50] "by proving one's
ability to *create* something special, a gold watch, banknotes, a
stamp collection, a diploma, or a title. . . . [but] the dignity of
man depends on creating and not on possessing."

The myth of power is also at the root of one of the most
characteristic facts of modern social development: the cultivation
of the masses, the rise of the masses. Here again we find a tendency which at present is not peculiar to one party but is common
to all of them. It is that same fear of being crushed, which leads
a free economy to organize itself in increasingly larger trusts,
just as the workers combine in increasingly disciplined masses.
The infinite variety and originality of men is absorbed into this
universal leveling process which dehumanizes them. It is striking
to observe how terribly lonely these men are in the midst of these
anonymous masses, which they have helped to shape because
they were afraid of being left alone in the battle of life. And since
these masses bear within themselves the inexorable law of power,
they must inevitably turn against each other in a struggle which

is infinitely more destructive than the individual struggles in times past. But the worst of all, perhaps, is not this clash of the masses, but rather the destruction of human personhood within the masses themselves.

This is the tragedy described by Arthur Koestler[78] in his book, *Darkness at Noon,* when he shows his hero, Rubashov, being crushed by the same principles of party discipline which he had publicly advocated and of which his executioners are just as much victims as he. "All he had believed in, fought for and preached during the last forty years," writes the author, "swept over his mind in an irresistible wave. The individual was nothing, the Party was all; the branch which broke from the tree must wither." And we all know that a similar book could be written about capitalism, which has undoubtedly sacrificed to its inflexible law as many capitalists as proletarians.

The same development has occurred in the realm of politics and statesmanship. We find the myth of power acting as a deep motivation in the formation of the great modern states. And their misfortune is precisely that they are too large, despite all the fallacious theories about poor and rich nations. Moreover, just as in the case of individuals, it is sometimes the richest who make the strongest and loudest demands, because they still consider themselves too poor. It is the great size of modern states that is the cause of their inner misery, because a gigantic centralized administration is no longer in accord with the human scale, and it is also the cause of their external ills, for the great states are almost fatally led to enter into increasingly vaster conflicts.

I want, however, to guard against Swiss pharisaism; for I know that the period in our history which is glorified in our schools and at our patriotic festivals is that in which the military strength and the territorial growth of our country flourished. A note of praise of the peaceful mission of modern Switzerland and the Red Cross is usually tacked on, doubtless quite sincerely. And yet I know very well that we owe our privilege of being a small country not so much to our love of peace as to our internal divisions and the weaknesses of our federated form of government, which put a stop to Switzerland's pursuit of political power.

The need to be powerful over against foreign countries, which has pushed most states in the direction of a many-tentacled centralization, has also reduced the small communities, which once were living cells, to the impersonal role of being mere administrative divisions.

But by a curious turn of events in this modern world, which believes that it has repressed the moral and the spiritual, the most grave consequence of the rise of the masses has been, not economic or political, but rather moral and spiritual. I want to speak of the criminal effect of propaganda, its powerful influence upon the whole world, and the universal misuse of this instrument of power.

Those men in the last century who dreamed of the blessing that would come to humanity through education were undoubtedly sincere. They imagined that man, if only he could read and write, would refine his personal judgment and achieve moral independence and spiritual maturity. Who could have foreseen that on the contrary we would be in our present situation, namely, in the triumph of the kind of thinking which is aimed at selfish goals, simplified into a slogan, co-ordinated and regimented, and, despite all logical objections, imposed upon men by massive repetition? It is not education that gives us freedom of thought, but rather spiritual experience.

It is really strange how incurious man is when it comes to recognizing and accepting a thought foreign to his own. It is not only the people of nations in which propaganda is an officially established instrument of government who know of their neighboring countries only what their authorities wish to tell them. Even people who live in an atmosphere of freedom like ours are quite content with one-sided news reports which are far more narrow and parochial than they were in centuries past. Since the great mass of people read one and the same newspaper day after day and this newspaper is obliged to say what will please its readers and also to say it in terms that are simple enough to give them the illusion that it is true, public information has arrived at an incredible impoverishment of thought and freedom of thought. Even Protestants allow themselves to be informed about Catholicism only through the medium of Protestant propaganda and vice versa. And we see entire, or almost entire, nations swallowing the same ideas and then being surprised and indignant that another nation should advocate just the opposite with the same unanimity. Each one protests against the cunning of the other's propaganda and then turns around and uses this protestation as an instrument of controlled and co-ordinated propaganda. Does not each one of us have his little ministry of propaganda?

Then when the sudden awakening and the cruel disillusionment come we hear people say (as I did recently in Germany): "All propaganda is lies." But all propaganda, like morphine, creates the need for more. People have so accustomed themselves to receiving their ideas from others that they are completely lost when the loudspeaker is silenced. They are already fat prey waiting for the next propagandist. Dr. Arnault Tzanck[23] writes: "Today propaganda, that false witness multiplied and modernized, assails man from his childhood."

C. G. Jung,[6] the psychiatrist, in an interview following the armistice that determined the destiny of Germany, attempted to give a psychological explanation of the Nazi atrocities. He gave a historical interpretation which approximates what I have been saying here. He recalled the ancient concept of demons which has long been believed to be outworn and then pointed out that Europe had claimed that it had driven out the demons through science. But he also reminded us of what the gospel says, that when the demons are driven out, they go where they are perhaps even more dangerous, more dangerous because they are no longer recognized as demons. He also pointed out that the masses are their chosen culture medium. "The power of the demons is prodigious," he said, "and the modern instruments of mass suggestion such as the press, radio, and films are at their service."

The same thing that happened to the Germans could happen to the Swiss, who are so proud of their intellectual independence, if they were a nation of eighty million people. And finally he recalled to mind the historical truth that the victor always runs the danger of being infected by the defeated. This is undoubtedly one of the tragedies of our time. Nazism has been beaten down, but it has taught the world to imitate its methods. In order to break the power of its propaganda it was necessary to adopt its weapons and to introduce in almost all countries a state propaganda, to which people, rather strangely, accommodated themselves, considering that in the past they had rebelled against the influence of the church.

But the church itself is in danger. In this world, broken and torn apart by conflicting ideologies, the temptation is very great to present Christianity as another ideology, to want it too to be strong, for God's sake, to marshal the masses, not—as Jung indicated—by the evangelical method of winning men "one by one," but rather resorting to propaganda and thinking like tacticians, strategists, and statisticians. But the propaganda demands that the gospel be simplified, that only its successes be presented in order to make it more persuasive, that its mysteries and difficulties be hidden; and all this is justified by the mass goal which is to be attained while reproaching other Christians for abandoning the world to its horrible fate. "These people," one of my colleagues writes to me, "are so full of their Christianity that they would like to make a system of government out of it by means of which we could instantly transform our world into a kingdom of God. The others think that in himself man is nothing but sin, that only Christ is at work in this world and that he knows his own. . . . and as we wait . . . let us tremble . . . for we are incapable of doing any good. It would seem that we are dancing on a tightrope between these two extremes."

Thus we find also in the church that same conflict of which we have been speaking and which is the malady of modern times. It is not my intention to criticize either one or the other of these two tendencies within the bosom of the church, but rather to show that the dispute between them is useless and to appeal for a synthesis: a church which will come out of its retreat, which will again speak in behalf of God, which will show that its message concerns all of life, politics, economics, and science, just as much as theology; and yet a church which guards against letting itself be infected by the modern demon of propaganda.

The modern myth of power has gravely impoverished our civilization. It has deprived it of all values that lie beyond the search for power. The beautiful, the good, the true cannot be weighed and measured. True knowledge is spiritual knowledge, which is beyond the reach of the world of quantity and therefore is disregarded by our civilization. "It has been proved," wrote Brunschwicg, "that knowing is measuring." So far, so good! But this is the very thing that so lamentably narrows the horizon of modern man. Whatever he cannot measure is simply discounted. "To what extent is a historical personality, an event, a work of art measurable?" asks Raymond Charmet.[8] And Charles Péguy explains: "Man will always prefer to measure himself than to see himself."

I have already mentioned the artists, the poets, the sensitive, the emotional people, the people who are tender and delicate of soul, whom modern society crushes and paralyzes by its scorn, the people who are coming in increasing numbers to the psychiatrist's office. It grieves me to see so many genuine values reduced to a vegetative life outside the mainstream of the world, so many values, far more precious than tons of oil, for which the world thirsts without knowing it, but which it nevertheless rejects and undervalues so cruelly that these very people are filled with inferiority feelings in the presence of an industrialist or a banker.

And how many people today cherish in their innermost heart the certainty that faith is the supreme value and still do not dare to confess it for fear of appearing to be weak! So greatly has religion been devaluated for us by presenting it as a refuge for the weak! And the persistent absence of strong men has resulted in our churches' being populated for the most part with those who are victims of society, with women, and the sick.

It is true that Francis of Assisi was physically weak. In the words of Pius IX, he had "just enough body to sustain his soul." It is true that Pascal and Vinet were wavering, tormented, weak men, measured by the scale of quantitative power which is in vogue today. But they had an entirely different kind of force, a far greater power, which, of course, is not measured by its victories over others: the strength to recognize their own weakness and rely upon God, the strength to respect others and help them to become stronger, instead of taking advantage of their weakness.

The most tragic effect of the myth of power is that it turns man away from an honest recognition of his weakness and pitches him into an illusory confidence in his own strength. And this self-confidence robs him of the strength of faith, which alone can break through the vicious circle of fear in which his pursuit of power keeps him enclosed.

I believe that I can discern in young people today signs of a revolution more profound than any we have known. The other revolutions were in the last analysis only advances in the same direction which our society had been pursuing for three hundred years. Weary of intellectual, economic, and ideological strife, these young people betray a yearning for the eternal and universal values, for art, for high thinking, for the spirit. May this young generation persuade the world that its fanatical pursuit of power was a utopian dream. And may it give back to the world an ideal of harmony and the precedence of values which is in conformity with the order of creation.

CHAPTER VI

The Task of the Church

[I WOULD BE able to cite here, as at the beginning of Chapter IV, many events which have occurred since the time when I wrote this book and which are inevitably apparent by their absence from these pages. But this would also show that the evolution of things, within the church as well as outside of it, has actually developed in the direction which I was calling for when the book was first written, and to a degree almost beyond my hopes. This is especially true of the idea of a rapprochement between Christians, not only within the churches allied to each other in ever greater numbers in the World Council of Churches of Geneva and New York, but also under the impulse of Popes John XXIII and Paul VI and the Vatican Council, in the Roman Catholic Church. The same is true of the "lay movements," the Evangelical Academies, the meetings of various professions, and the international and interconfessional sessions of "the medicine of the person," which has continued to affirm itself.—P.T., February, 1964.]*

First the diagnosis, then the therapy.

Sometimes, of course, the problems of diagnosis are so fascinating that we are tempted to discuss them for their own sake. But a genuine doctor never loses sight of his essential goal. His only concern in establishing a correct diagnosis is to institute an effective treatment. So in examining the thorny questions which the sick world presents to our spirit, it has not been an academic

---

* The author has furnished this introductory note for the English version of this book. (Trans.)

predilection for dialectics that has prompted us to do so. The anguish of the world today is so poignant, the accumulated suffering so flagrant, the threat of the immediate future so grave, that only the heart should lead us. And we wish to put at its service all the faculties of our mind.

At the very outset I confessed the difficulties of the diagnosis. The difficulty of treatment is certainly even greater. Not many of my readers would exchange places with the statesmen today, and no more would I! And yet the sickness of the world is not only a sickness of the whole organism; it touches every cell, every one of us. Its healing depends upon our own personal healing.

It is therefore with conviction and enthusiasm that I wish to attempt to sketch the outlines of a genuine treatment as I see it. Often the physician, for want of a specific and causal therapy, is obliged to confine himself to the treatment of symptoms. This is quite generally the case in the field of public life today. Because the ills are so urgent, governments in all countries are compelled to improvise measures which will prevent the worst from happening. Such precipitate measures, however, can sometimes be harmful to the patient; in no case can they relieve us from searching with all our heart for the cause of the ill and its treatment.

If it is true that the cause of catastrophes lies in the rift, which for several centuries now has torn asunder two inseparable realities, the material and the spiritual, in the individual as well as in society, then the cure can come only from their reintegration. Only God, who created man as body, soul, and spirit, can effect this harmonious synthesis in us and in society. Without him, we may be able somehow to co-ordinate our economic measures, our imaginative efforts, our intellectual conclusions, and our spiritual aspirations, but we cannot fuse them into an organic whole.

It is my conviction that the church's hour has come. The church instituted by God, the servant of God, must again become his instrument to effect the synthesis for which all men of our time are consciously or unconsciously yearning. And here I mean the church in the broadest sense, not only the clergy, not only the established churches, but all those who have been gripped by Jesus Christ.

I believe that I can discern many signs that the hour of the church has come.

First, the breath of moderation that is stirring in the scientific world today, which is in singular contrast with the smug pride and facile optimism of the last century. Here is an example. One of the masters of French surgery, Dr. R. Leriche,[79] professor in the Collège de France, writes in his most recent book: "As soon as we try to understand the secret springs of illnesses, we find that the books give us only superficial explanations, which are sometimes childish, with little or nothing behind them. . . ." And it is one of the masters of medicine in my country, Professor Roch, who quotes this statement in the *Revue médicale de la Suisse romande.* One would certainly not have read a statement like this at the beginning of the century!

Today's physicists, the most scientific of all the scientists, who must grapple with the fantastic and unfathomable problems raised by the quantum theory, are also the ones who have become the most modest. Until recently they were accustomed to speaking of their discipline as an exact science par excellence and of looking down upon the biological and social sciences as being governed by laws that were merely statistical. But the further they advance in their researches the more clearly do they see that physical and mathematical laws are also statistical laws and that, far from being "exact," their conclusions are rather on the order of multiple possibilities, between which one can choose only on the basis of arbitrary and uncertain convention. I am thinking of the dissertation written by my nephew, Pierre Bouvier,[80] for his doctorate in natural sciences. To be sure, I do not understand a single line of its mathematical development with all its conventional symbols. But I do understand the incalculable philosophical importance of these works of the specialists. They are upsetting our conceptions of the world and more than ever before reintroducing the idea of mystery at the very moment when the scientists of the past dreamed their successors would banish all mystery from the horizon of their thinking.

The hour of the church, the hour in which the intellectual elite in all disciplines turns away from the fallacious hope of a golden age of science. The hour when it is being discovered on every side that the more human knowledge accumulates the more numerous, mysterious, and inexhaustible become the problems it presents to the mind.

I have spoken of the boldness with which, not many years ago, Freud thought it possible to derive from his newly discovered science a definitive explanation of religion, philosophy, and poetry, which he proposed to reduce to simple psychic functions. And I have shown that already his most faithful disciples have been obliged to depart from him on this central point and recognize that the world of true spiritual values eludes psychological analysis.

I have given many quotations in this book, more than would comport with a book that is to be merely pleasing. But my aim is a different one; my purpose in including these quotations has been to show that today men of very different outlooks, doctors, lawyers, economists, scientists, writers, freethinkers, atheists, Jews, as well as Catholic and Protestant Christians are searching for something completely new. For something which is not simply a prolongation of the cultural development of the last several centuries, but which will rather interrupt that development. For something which is not so much on the order of scientific analysis but is more on the order of intuitive analysis; for something which no longer fragments man but rather restores his unity.

The hour of the church. These men, like Dr. Menkès, Dr. Tzanck, Dr. Baruk, Lecomte du Noüy, or Henri Bergson do not, of course, speak like people who grew up in the church. Indeed, we traditional Christians often have difficulty in coming to an understanding and agreement with them. Nevertheless, there is a strange concordance in all their aspirations, and obviously their search is a religious search, to which only the church of Christ will be able to respond. But, in order to do this, the church will have to open its heart, learn from these men, and remember the words of its Master: "Many will come from east and west . . ."[81] But it must guard itself against repeating the words of Nathaniel, "Can any good come out of Nazareth?"[82]

I am convinced that we today, we Christians, must unite two things which are often opposed but which Christ joined together. On the one hand we must have a clear consciousness of our own unique vocation, our calling to make His voice heard, that voice which alone can provide a true answer to the questions of this tormented world. But at the same time we must guard against making His divine person the subject of division between us and other men, against rejecting them under the pretext that they do not possess the truth which has been given to us. Without concealing anything of our faith, let us seek that which brings us closer to them, that common need for a spiritual renewal, even though they may put it in words different from ours.

Will the church of Christ be equal to its task in the face of this disquietude of our contemporaries? Will it be able to bring about not a discussion which rebuffs it but rather a living dialogue and fellowship which responds to their confused yearnings? That is the question that haunts me.

Professor Viktor von Weizsäcker recently told me that at a convention of psychoanalysts he had addressed this question to Dr. C. G. Jung: "What, in your opinion, is the essence of neurosis?" And the answer was: "Neurotics are all searching for religion."

Have we not seen that the modern world is acting like a neurotic? Dr. Jung does not claim to be a Christian. But he sees, far better than many Christians, the true meaning of the anxiety of our time. I am always amazed to hear so many ministers complain of the religious indifference of our contemporaries. "How do you manage," they ask me, "to get those with whom you talk to interest themselves in religious problems?" I have no answer to that question. I do not need to stir up any religious disquietude in my patients. I know that they are full of it already and far more consciously than they admit. If we look upon them as being indifferent, we are not establishing between them and us the climate in which they will disclose their real torment. Let us be the first to discern what modern man is seeking.

He is thirsting for God. "The aggrandized body is waiting for a supplementation of the soul," wrote Henri Bergson, "and . . . mechanicalism requires a mysticism." The question is whether the religion which is now to be given to men is the true one. Otherwise they will go on inventing new religions which will inevitably break down one after another. Everybody today is searching for an answer to those problems to which science pays no attention: the problem of their destiny, the mystery of evil, the question of death. I am not saying that the church of today is not answering these questions. The trouble is that the answers are being given in terms which our contemporaries no longer understand. These people use a completely different language to express their personal and social difficulties, a concrete, direct kind of language which the church must adopt if it is to make itself understood. As the world was despiritualizing itself the church has been disincarnating, disembodying itself. Hence there is a tremendous misunderstanding, which undoubtedly is just as much the fault of the church as of the world. "The number of people," writes Lecomte du Noüy,[32] "who . . . do not find the answer in religion, who are searching in despair, is considerable. . . . We cannot say that the church has dealt brilliantly with the problems which arose from the industrial revolution."

To be sure, if the world does not listen to the church, this is often because it does not want to listen to God, against whom it has rebelled. And yet the church justifies itself all too easily if it thinks that the fault lies only in the world and not in itself. Since we are now searching for a treatment, let us again take up Dr. Maeder's case and see how the doctor proceeded. There too it was easy for the father to reproach his son for his rebellion, to denounce his vanity and his bragging, and to demand his submission. The doctor, however, made it his business to understand the boy. Soon the boy confessed his inner confusion, but he added that his father had deceived him and that his deception had dealt him a terrible blow. It had shaken his confidence in the moral ideal which his father had taught him. Then the picture became more sharply defined: what disillusioned the son was that the father did nothing about the unjust criticism that was leveled against his mother. Accordingly, it was the lack of unity between the parents that initiated the son's rebellion. What drove him to reject their moral principles was the fact that they betrayed themselves by their dissension, by their lack of mutual love.

We may compare the church with these parents and modern man with their rebellious son. The story teaches us that it was the inner division of the church and its faults which contributed most to modern man's estrangement from Christianity. The father, whose tragic story Dr. Maeder tells, lost all authority over his son because he himself did not follow the moral of love which he prescribed for his son, because he had no real understanding with his wife. In the same way the church has compromised its influence upon the world by its own inner dissensions.

The psychologist cannot forgo remarking here that the discussions which bring our two great Christian churches into opposition are astonishingly similar to those which he finds in marital conflicts. In married couples the vehemence of their mutual reproaches very often lies in the affection that binds them together. If they were indifferent to each other, they would not attack with such passion every view of the other partner that was different from their own. Lovers' quarrels! To be sure, between married partners, just as between our churches, there may sometimes be disputes over fundamental, essential things; but these play a secondary role compared with the emotional factors which separate the couple. It is mainly jealousy, spite, injured self-esteem, suspicion, or lack of honesty that stir up the conflict. And often-times, by way of the phenomenon of rationalization, the dispute over ideas appears to them to be the cause of their emotional conflict rather than the result of it. Between a couple who are bound together by genuine love all differences of opinion concerning fundamental things find their solution; or, if their opinions on certain points remain opposed, they at least respect those of the other party and guard against stubbornly condemning them. On the other hand, where there is an emotional tension between them, this continues to foment and envenom the dispute over ideas and opinions. It is affectivity, emotion, passion, that separates people.

I am not disregarding the importance of the theological problems raised by a *rapprochement* between Catholicism and Protestantism. But these differences are by no means sufficient to explain the blind mutual prejudice that all too often prevails between Protestants and Catholics. And a solution of these controversies over faith and doctrine would undoubtedly be found if we could overcome our passions.

In any case, I want to guard against limiting the question of the unity of the church solely to the relations between the two great Christian confessions. Thousands of dogmatic and ecclesiological nuances separate the Orthodox, the Lutherans, Anglicans, the Reformed, and others. Within Protestantism many small communions fanatically insist that they are in sole possession of the truth. And behind the apparent unity of the Roman church there is room for all kinds of theological disputes.

The doctor often observes that a Protestant converts to Catholicism, a Catholic converts to Protestantism, or a member of one of these great churches converts to some sect or other, not so much because of theological reasons, as he himself thinks, but rather because of a quarrel he has had with his family or with a clergyman. And above all, this doctor sees that beween Christians, just as between married couples, the argument never ceases, because each one denounces the faults of the other, instead of recognizing his own, because we preach forgiveness but seldom practice it.

Let us remember that the Reformers did not wish to found a new church, but rather to reform the existing church. And we will know that it is not being unfaithful to them to seek ways and means of finding a *rapprochement* between the various confessions. In any case, by their development the Roman church and Protestant churches are manifestly striving toward the same goal.

Dr. Joseph Zwiebel,[43] a Jewish doctor who was converted to Christianity, shows us clearly that Jews and Christians are perfectly right in the reproaches they address to each other. And yet he also shows that these mutual reproaches are not only sterile but also a great obstacle to the conversion of the Jews.

We have seen that Dr. Maeder spoke to the parents of his patient. He helped them to see that estrangement was one of the important causes of their son's crisis. He urged them to examine themselves and to come closer together. In the same way, it seems to me that if the hour of the church is striking today, it must above all be an hour of a great movement toward inner reconciliation. Goethe wrote: "It is a law of spirits and specters that they must go out by the way they came in." The modern specter of unbelief came in by way of the rent that had been torn in the unity of the church.

It is true, of course, that there were divisions among men in the ancient world and the Middle Ages. But these have assumed enormous proportions in modern times. Now everything is nothing but one great struggle between states and groups of states, between social classes, between competitors. The great problem of our time is to restore men's faith in a solidarity that transcends all differences of opinion. The world will not listen to the church so long as it does not successfully apply itself to the resolving of its own divisions. The church can give this demonstration and doubtless it will give it; for only a spiritual unity can be both solid and respectful of the conventions of others. Here again the situation is like that of marital conflicts. A true reconciliation never takes place unless there is a movement of the Spirit. Only the Spirit is able to establish a bond which allows each to be faithful to himself. Harmony is only an illusion if it results in the tyranny of one partner over the other or if the two must avoid every controversial subject simply to get along with each other.

The unity of the church, which I—and many other Christians— call for today, will be a spiritual unity. There will be no sentimental embraces that gloss over the difficulties, nor a utopian search for complete agreement in theological views, for intellectual discussions separate more often than they unite. But if the modern world is so terribly divided, it is because it has lost that supremacy of the Spirit of which we have spoken, that spiritual bond that transcends and harmonizes the elements of diversity without impugning their proper character and vocation. The church can and must give a demonstration of this kind of unity.

Let the Catholics be truly Catholic, let the Protestants be truly Protestant, let the members of the Salvation Army be true warriors for salvation! But let spiritual unity be established among all Christians! Then the world will return to the church to seek the secret of a cure of its ills.

It is an impressive thing to read the homage which Dr. Zwiebel, the Jewish physician, pays to four of his fellow prisoners who were Catholics: a doctor, a doctor who was a priest, a priest, and a dentist. They truly revealed Christ and the Christian life to him. But they were so completely free of party spirit that, even though they were all Catholics, the new convert received Christian baptism in the Protestant church.

To restore the unity of the church will require more today than a pious wish. The development of the ecumenical movement, and the course which it has taken are signs of the times in which we find serious reasons for hope. Indeed, the Ecumenical Council of the church has guarded against its becoming a kind of diplomatic conference. It has not yielded to the temptation of formal compromise, nor has it prevented any church from being faithful to itself, nor failed in its task of establishing a true unity among them. Its method was defined by its general secretary, Dr. Vissert 't Hooft at the inauguration of the Ecumenical Institute in Bossey. Its purpose is not to federate the churches, but rather "to free the Church of Jesus Christ within the churches of men." And the attitude of the Roman Church itself, which sent a message of good will to the Council on the occasion of its session in Geneva likewise shows that the hour of Christian unity is drawing near.

In order to define this task more precisely, let us go back once more to Dr. Maeder's account. After showing us what the mutual relations of the parents were, he goes on to show us the way to a *rapprochement* between them and their son with a view to his cure, which is comparable to a right attitude of the church toward the world and its sufferings.

Unfortunately, when we are confronted with the task of treating a young neurotic we often see that the behavior of his parents toward him, though understandable, only aggravates his difficulties. This is the case especially when they criticize and judge him. Thus in Dr. Maeder's case the father could quite justly say to his son: "You are sick because you are revolting against me. If you would listen to me, if you did not keep rejecting all the principles I taught you, if you would work instead of dreaming about jazz, you would not be so tormented. You had better watch out; you are on the wrong path, and if you keep on you will make a mess of your whole life." But that kind of talk generally succeeds only in driving the adolescent deeper into his revolt and neurosis.

We would therefore be on the wrong track if we were to assume the attitude of a judge of our world today. To condemn the world under the pretext of converting it is a dangerous temptation of believers. This is not the perspective from which I have written this book, and if I have given that impression, I beg the reader's pardon. I declare what I believe to be true, namely, that the sufferings of humanity come from its estrangement from faith. But this means that humanity is a victim, that it is sick, and we must have compassion for the sufferings of humanity and bear with them in faith. And if there is fault, then it is the fault of all of us, the believers as well as the unbelievers, perhaps even more on the part of us who have faith.

Rather we must understand. Even in the atheistic invectives of the Marxists, the Nazis, the Nietzscheans, and the existentialists, there is the expression of a deep, inner sadness, which ought to call forth our love for them. Who would dare to reply to Karl Marx that religion has never served as opium or to Sartre that we have never feigned love instead of truly loving?

There is not one part which is Christianity and another which is antichristian, nor a battle between the two. We do not embody Christianity any more than the father of the neurotic adolescent represented Christianity and possessed the right simply to say to him: "Return to me." Such an attitude can only strengthen the world in its prejudices against the church. A truly spiritual movement is not born either from argument or from reproaches. It springs up when God intervenes. Then everybody, equally bruised, is driven to self-examination.

The world is sick and suffering. Let us therefore regard it with understanding and love. Let us remember the words of Ignatius Loyola: "Be sweet and gentle with those who are nervous." This is the same attitude which Karl Barth, the Protestant theologian, defined in his book on Europe; and yet no one has suspected Barth of not fighting for the truth.

In a small brochure Dr. Jean de Rougemont[83] tells in a moving way how the physician is suddenly enabled to comprehend what human misery means the moment he becomes conscious of his own misery. As long as he remains merely the scientist, the honored, influential man, who has a "case" before him, he can give good advice, but he does not touch the man at the point of his real distress. And yet it can happen that he may recall an hour in his life in which he really had no reason to be proud of himself. Then he realizes that all this prestige of knowledge, titles, and social recognition is only a mask behind which he is hiding his own misery. Then he really feels that he is the brother of this sick person before him, and he finds the way to his heart.

A hospital chaplain told us that sometimes he has pitied the sick people who are visited by one after another of certain pious and charitable souls, members of various communions, who come for the purpose of converting them. To the sick people it appears that, far from sympathizing with their sufferings, these persons are taking advantage of the fact that they are confined to bed, weak, and incapable of replying, in order to indoctrinate them. Their pious visitors derive a great satisfaction from this; they have found an opportunity to exercise their zeal. Sometimes they even use the patient's illness as an argument to persuade him. They keep talking to him with great fervor and never think of listening to him. In reality they are enjoying themselves without realizing the domination they are exercising in this unequal battle.

Unfortunately, the will to power quickly insinuates itself even into a spiritual ministry. None of us escapes it. And yet there is no graver hindrance to a true movement of the Spirit than spiritual imperialism. Let us not forget the severity with which Christ condemned the proselytism of the Pharisees.

Let us also not forget that it was precisely the spiritual imperialism of the church at the end of the Middle Ages which provoked that sharp reaction of which we have been speaking, namely, the repression of the spiritual. And even today the church would alienate the world if it were to take advantage of its sufferings in order to bring it under its domination, to impose a system of thought upon it, and take a dialectic revenge upon it.

Christianity is not one ideology over against other ideologies. It is a life inspired by the Holy Spirit. Its victories are nothing but victories over itself, not over others. It propagates itself through humility and self-examination, not through triumphs.

Therefore if we want to help the world in its present crisis, then we Christians dare no longer give the impression that we believe there are two opposing camps: the Christian, to which we belong, and that of the atheistic ideologies, our opponents. We must stop saying to them: Come back to us, for we possess the truth. We must rather say: Let us all turn back to Christ. "It ill becomes us," wrote Péguy, "to play the self-righteous ones."

This spirit of our century, whose main characteristics we have pointed out, has invaded the church itself. It too has allowed itself to be won over to that optimistic confidence in man and his progress, to the myth of power, to faith in numbers and statistics, and that hypertrophic enlargement of the "intellectual story" of the human personality, that repression of the conscience in the face of social misery.

When Pierre Hervé[1] writes, "The first thing that is demanded of Communists is humanity . . . [that is, that] he immerse himself in the mass of men, know their needs and their cares . . . ," then we recognize what the church should have done long before the Communists. When Nietzsche writes, "The good people have always been the beginning of the end," we must recognize that the moralism, which Christ so severely condemned, has seriously permeated the church. When Professor Jacques Ellul[52] writes, "Man lives in a materialistic civilization; and not only in Russia, where a materialistic philosophy prevails, but in the entire world," then again we must confess that the church has in large measure come to terms with the power of money. Thus Pastor Henri Ochsenbein,[46] after vigorously denouncing the materialism of the modern secular world devotes a no less severe chapter to the "religious materialism" of the men of the church. When a leading Communist says to Ellul,[52] "We are sick of hearing about human dignity, the rights of man, respect for personality," then again we must confess that the church itself has contributed to the devaluation of these watchwords by repeating them ad nauseam without teaching its members to apply them in their social life.

And finally, with regard to individualism, that great plague of modern times, which plunges man into dreadful solitude, we recognize that it is especially prevalent in the church. The church is far from presenting a picture of true community, like that of the primitive church. It is very far from being that "absolute organism,"[31] that perfect society, of which Charles Secrétan spoke, in which he wished that secular society would find an eloquent example of harmonious relationships between the individual person and the collective whole.

When I use the word "church," I do not mean a vague and abstract idea, but each one of us Christians, all participating in this great schism between the spiritual and the temporal. We piously preserve the spiritual truths of the gospel, but we no longer see all the practical demands that they make upon us in our material and professional life. These inconsistencies of Christians are plain for everybody to see. They are the main cause of the world's disaffection with regard to Christ, and it is certainly not for us to read a lecture to our contemporaries.

One Sunday afternoon when I was on military service I found myself alone with my commandant, a doctor like myself. All of our comrades in the officers' mess were on leave. We took our coffee into a beautiful garden overlooking a splendid panorama of mountains. Suddenly and in a quite unexpected way, my chief told me what his feelings were toward me. "When I was advised several weeks ago that you had been assigned to my unit," he said, "I thought to myself: What am I going to do with this Holy Joe, this pious bigot? I never dreamed that you would so quickly become one of my best friends!" The way was open for a deeper conversation. As if he wanted to answer a question I had not asked, he began to explain the reasons for his hostility toward Christians. Then came anecdotes from his life as a doctor: a visit he made in the luxurious apartment of a pious family highly regarded in the church, next to a domestic servant who had been lying seriously ill and without care for several days in a small, windowless attic room. A married couple whom he had treated, where the devout wife exercised such a cruel, jealous tyranny over her poor husband that their married life was literally poisoned. Clothed in her virtue, she implacably prosecuted him in court for having sought consolation elsewhere.

I made no reply. I know very well that all these things a doctor sees behind the scenes of seemingly respectable society. Then came some scandalous stories about clergymen. For several hours my friend continued his indictment. That evening he took me to a neighboring village where we dined privately. He now began to tell me about his own unhappiness. Then I asked him: Do you have any other solution for the injustices of the world except the power of Christ, this power which can make a Christian as well as an unbeliever examine himself, which can compel him to acknowledge his offenses and make amends for them? And I in turn told him some anecdotes, stories about others and about myself, of what can happen when the Spirit stirs and moves. A few weeks later when this officer received orders to open a military hospital, he came to me and said, "Listen here, I am organizing a banquet for this dedication, but I want something more than that. Go find a minister for me and ask him to come and bless this house. You can explain it to him better than I can. He doesn't need to say very much, but I want our men to know that nothing good can be done here below without God's benediction."

When the hour of the church strikes, this is the hour not only of the humbling of the world, but also of the humbling and profound transformation of the church.

I should like now to define more clearly one aspect of this transformation as I see it. Our age is suffering because of the rift between the spiritual and the temporal. It is suffering not only because of the despiritualization of the world, but also because of the disincarnation of the church. The church, it seems to me, has separated itself from real life and thus simply abandoned the world to its practical difficulties and taken refuge in an ivory tower. And for this it bears a heavy responsibility for our present crisis. True, it still goes on preaching, but far from the public place where the practical life of men is lived. "Morality is not a theory which one proves," writes Dr. Zwiebel,[43] "but rather a

life that one demonstrates by living." And then, speaking of all
the social and intellectual struggles that throbbed within his heart
and mind, he goes on to say: "My generation, which was shaped
and matured between the two world wars . . . was dominated
above all by political movements which were for the most part
far removed from Christianity." The world in which he lived was
"a world in which Jesus was absent." I am reminded also of
what Péguy said about Christians: "Their hands are clean, but
they have no hands."

Our religion is the religion of the incarnation and we have all
too often forgotten this. The world had to face tremendous tasks.
The industrial revolution, the era of science, the progress of technology, the enormous development of economic needs, the formation of the great masses, and many other factors have had tragic
repercussions. It was necessary to improvise measures in order to
prevent the worst from happening. Mistakes were made, it is
true, but countless men of good will at least tried to do something; often, in spite of the fact that their doctrines were wrong,
they performed arduous work and gave an example of great
devotion to the service of a tormented, broken world. In all these
political, social, economic, and cultural efforts the church played
almost no part. It was indifferent to the world and left it to be a
prey to its own problems. It took refuge in the spiritual domain;
not that it should neglect this sphere, but that it should also seek
there for practical solutions for the organization of society and the
orientation of culture.

Thus if the church must humble itself, it must also speak out;
it must clearly formulate what the gospel means for economic,
political, and intellectual life. It must formulate, as is being said
today, an evangelical, professional, and social ethics, which still
remains almost entirely to be discovered.

And here too we see some very promising signs on the horizon.

Some years ago there was established in Geneva a Protestant
study center, which now comprises nine sections. It provides
living encounters between theologians and men of different pro-

fessions: doctors, lawyers, economists, artists, and so on. It offers the opportunity to compare our points of view, and it has been through our participation in it that we have begun to realize how much the church has needed just such an institution. Thus, for example, as between doctors and theologians, we have one and the same object of study, namely, the human person; whereas hitherto we had practically no contact whatsoever. In fact we were even full of mutual prejudices. We doctors accused the theologians of being separated from reality, of preaching beautiful principles but without telling us how to apply them in the daily circumstances of our profession. They on the other hand were afraid that our physiological and psychological study of human behavior would cause men to throw overboard all consciousness of sin. Now we are just beginning a truly common search for the fundamental facts of a Christian medicine. We physicians see very clearly that we cannot find any right concept of man, of sickness, or of death without the help of the theologians. And they too see clearly that they no longer have any right to feel that they are above the burning questions which present themselves to us every day.

It is easy to imagine the number and the gravity of the problems with which the section for economists or the one for lawyers is confronted. These meetings are just as profitable to the theologians as to their fellow discussants. They startle them out of the moral solitude in which they have enclosed themselves and for which they have been reproached. They will undoubtedly lead to a renewal of genuine pastoral care which has been so neglected, a pastoral care in which ministers who are fully aware of the difficulties of real life must help the faithful to master them.

In France too the Protestant professional associations have been arranging such meetings and likewise seeking to work out an evangelical ethics. In the Netherlands the war prompted the emergence of the movement called "Church and Society," a representative of which I recently met. "Hitler made us open our Bibles again," he said. Faced with an occupying power which was determined to derive directives for the whole of social life from its pagan ideology and to impose them on everybody, it was necessary for Christians to search the Bible not only for the promise of personal salvation but also for answers to actual questions which arose from day to day: Is this or that command of the occupation authorities compatible with the will of God revealed in the gospel or not?

On a number of occasions I have been in Germany with my wife at the invitation of the Evangelical Academy of Bad Boll. Here again one could observe that the terrible Nazi flood had produced a perhaps completely unexpected result, namely, that of forcing the church out of its reserve and obliging it again to accept its full responsibility to society. It was there that I was best able to gauge the seriousness of that rift between the church and the world which I have here described. One of my German colleagues said to me: "One day you may perhaps be thankful to us for having gone through this tragic experience, which had to be gone through in order to understand what this modern dream of building a society detached from its spiritual foundations can lead to." And another, alluding to the practice of euthanasia, added: "Medicine, which is called to save life, allowed itself to be forced to put its skills at the service of death. This could never have happened if it had not previously lost its Christian motivation."

Yes, the Nazi catastrophe was a sign of the bankruptcy of the modern ideal. The church had been shut up in its own chapels. It was tolerated provided that it made no further claim to govern society. Men believed that they could regulate society without any transcendental principle, purely on the basis of a science which proclaimed its moral neutrality. But under these circumstances it was possible for another power to arise which did not hesitate to bend law, medicine, education, and everything else to its pagan ethics.

After the catastrophe the German church, whose most eminent

representatives had been the first victims of the regime, understood this very well. There can be a fruitful transformation of the German people only if a new Christian elite is established, consecrated men who in every domain will apply themselves to the reconstruction of a society inspired by Christ.

To do this the church could not confine itself to preaching to its pious adherents within its church buildings. It established the Evangelical Academy of Bad Boll, to which it invited representatives of various vocations—lawyers, farmers, physicians, workers, educators, mayors, etc. These people live there in the community generally for a full week. They study the Bible with reference to their vocational and professional problems and social responsibilities; they discuss with theologians these problems and responsibilities in the light of the Bible.

I have taken part in meetings of doctors and artists and have learned much from them. In particular I have come to realize that, if my country was spared the great distress, it does not owe this to any particular merit of its own. What happened to Germany could have happened to us too, for all of us who participate in this civilization which is divorced from Christianity are responsible for the modern schism which opened the door for Nazism.

Evangelical academies similar to that at Bad Boll have now multiplied in Germany. And in other countries, too, movements similar to those which I have described in France, the Netherlands and Switzerland have come into being. At the Chateau de Bossey I took part in an international meeting of representatives of all these movements convened by the Ecumenical Council of Churches. It was the first small, modest nucleus of pioneers. But thanks to their common convictions and experiences, which united them beyond their national and confessional differences, they exhibited an astonishing unanimity. The Church as a whole is only beginning to assess the importance of this new orientation which seeks to put an end to the rift that separates it from the real world.

In its final resolution the conference at Bossey made this statement: "The first fact that impressed itself upon all was the profound unity of foundation and goal in all the national organizations represented. In the course of the war when it was not possible to establish any connection between the various countries the identical question arose in many of them and a similar answer was given to it. The question erupted from the situation of the church itself and its relation with the world. Everywhere men became aware that the process of secularization in the world was tending more and more to detach the laity from the church. Quite apart from those who have become completely absorbed by the circumambient paganism, it was observed that many of those who maintained a certain attachment to the church regarded it as a spiritual luxury, a refuge, not as the place where their whole existence was subjected to the command of God. Hence faith appeared to be a reality which had fewer and fewer points of contact with human life. The movements which we represent have sought to respond to this situation. They started from the certainty that the work of evangelization in the world today could no longer be confined to a simple exposition of the Christian faith nor to an emotional appeal to sentiment, but must rather seek to reach men in their real life and their everyday problems. These problems present themselves mainly within their vocational life. This is why the questionable movements have sought to operate within this framework."

I also participated with about thirty colleagues from six counties and five different denominations, again at Chateau de Bossey, in the first Week of Meditation and Study of "the medicine of the person." Physicians, surgeons, psychiatrists, and other specialists, professors and general practitioners there formed indefectible bonds with each other by sharing their experiences, their convictions, and the desire that animated them all, namely, to recover the sense of the human person in its wholeness and unity, to re-establish a person-to-person relationship between us and our patients which might satisfy their deepest needs, in order that medicine may become what God wills it to be; that was our endeavor. This at the same time implies a renewal in our medical thinking and a more complete spiritual consecration of our personal, family, and professional life.

The Catholic church on its part has also been going in the same direction in the founding of Catholic Action, in which in all countries it is putting emphasis upon the activity of the laymen in their professional and vocational life.

Then, finally, I have shown that everywhere men who are estranged from the church are beginning anew to pose the problem of man from the point of view of their various disciplines. Thus they are approaching the movement which is taking form in the churches. Therefore we are at the beginning of a new stage in which we may see the two parts into which human life has been torn for several centuries welded together again. When we think about it, it seems incredible that all this should appear so new. How could the church have become so indifferent to the world and its fate? How could the leaders of culture attempt to build a civilization without a knowledge of man? For that is where we are. How could they believe that one could practice medicine, direct the economy, write books, understand history and sociology without having a clear conception of man? Now science, the unchallenged master of the universities, has presumed to overturn the conception of man which is based upon the biblical revelation. And the concept which it finally arrives at, namely that man is an absurd and fortuitous agglomeration of electrons, is, according to public admission of even such a biologist as Jean Rostand,[17] literally untenable.

Thus today nobody is able to give a satisfactory answer to this simple question: What is man? No one, not even the church, has concerned himself about this for several centuries. Almost all of our contemporaries have a view of man which is far more Platonic than Christian, a view that sets a naturally immortal soul over against a body which has been reduced to the role of a transitory, noxious, contemptible garment. In a penetrating biblical study,

Dr. Edouard Schweizer[84] has also shown that "our current idea of death is more Hellenistic than biblical in origin" and that "sickness and death can become positive, rather than negative, for us," but only from the evangelical point of view of that "totally transcendent event, the cross and the resurrection."

How astonishing it is, under these conditions, that our doctors, historians, and sociologists do not see the primary role that the Spirit plays in the life of the individual and the collective life of man! For "the truth is," says Professor Leriche,[79] "that we have a habit of seeing only what we already know." People think we are revolutionary when we describe the most obvious facts which anybody can verify, for example, when we show that a sick person, even though the agent of his illness may be a known bacterium, has nevertheless fallen victim to it only because, tormented by pangs of conscience, he has lost all hope and wants to die.

For centuries science has been accumulating documents which show the importance of material factors in the history of the individual and society. Now with the same patience we must gather such data on the role of the spiritual factors. Otherwise we shall go on being condemned as we are today for not understanding man. Certainly it is not only the Marxists who hold a materialistic view of history. Even before the Marxists the positivists saw in history nothing more than a blind play of conflicting forces.

Thus today there lies before us an immense labor of thought which demands a close collaboration between theologians and the intellectuals of all disciplines.

But not only a labor of thought.

Just as we walk on two legs, I believe that we shall advance toward this new Christian culture which we need only through a combination of thought and experience. Thought without action means intellectualism and endless theological debate. Action without thought means improvisation and dependence on casual inspiration.

But if in the light of the Bible we recover a right view of man, it will lead us to new experiences and these in turn will become a more eloquent demonstration than the most scholarly exposition. Meetings like those at the Protestant study center or at Bad Boll will not really fulfill their purpose as long as they are only discussion circles and above all do not lead their participants to a personal experience of Jesus Christ which can transform them at the deepest level of their life. "Before we elaborate theories," writes Professor Ellul,[52] "before we set up economic doctrines, we must first have men. To provide men—this is the task of the church."

This rift between the spiritual and the temporal not only divides the world in general, it also disturbs the inner harmony of every single one of us. We need to close that gap within ourselves before we can help the world to do so. This is not only a matter of concepts and ideas, not only a question of the spiritual or the intellectual in the narrower sense, but rather of the lordship of Jesus Christ over our whole life.

The church must proclaim, but it must also show: show what happens when a businessman wants to be honest, when a physician really respects the human person, when an artist really seeks his inspiration in God, when a lawyer applies his faith in his profession. This means, now and always, a veritable revolution.

Even in our world today, deeply pagan as it is, every man can have a totally new experience as soon as he allows God to direct his real life and not merely to inspire his feelings. A new civilization will not spring full-grown from the brain of some theoretician. It will be built through the bold obedience of countless Christians. Men are all living in a narrow beaten track. They hardly ever subject what is hallowed by universal consent to conscientious examination. Whenever one of them departs from conventional habit, his example is contagious. But it takes a strong passion to provoke such an unusual step.

One such passion is the revolution that shakes our whole being when Jesus Christ takes possession of us; and yet a passion that

brings a person into harmony rather than throwing him into disorder. What is the meaning of that precedence of personhood of
which we spoke? What does it mean for us? Not simply our
adherence to a spiritual conception of the world and man, but
rather that we surrender our whole being to the authority of Jesus
Christ. This means that we must let God direct us in the use of
our body and our goods, our work and our money, as well as in
the realization of our feelings and our ideas. This is precisely
where the resolution of the "schism" lies. This means that our
devotion to Jesus Christ turns over to him not only our inner life
but also our social life; that day by day we seek in quiet meditation a divine inspiration for the details of our activity.

Here I must answer a question which is sometimes put to me:
What is the relation between the spirit and the Holy Spirit? In
this book I have often spoken of the spirit. I have shown that
from the Creation it has been the specific element in the human
being that makes him a person, essentially different from the
animal. It is a specific element, common to all men, whether they
are Christian or not, which bestows upon them a peculiar dignity, no matter whether they betray it or debase themselves. But
this spirit which ought to preside over and order our whole being
finds itself eclipsed and disfigured by the unchecked exercise of
our personal will. Despite all our efforts we can never by our own
power restore it to its original sovereignty as the "fine point" of
our personality. For that a new spirit must be given to us by God,
and this is the Holy Spirit.

Only inspired men—that is, men who accept the Holy Spirit as
they accept Jesus Christ as their Lord—can truly contribute to the
restoration of the precedence of the spirit in the world. The
church believes in the Holy Spirit, but it puts little emphasis
upon its importance. In the same way that God became incarnate
in history in Jesus Christ, so he also becomes incarnate in us
through the Holy Spirit. He exercises an influence upon our body
as well as our spirit, upon every one of our cells as well as our
feelings.

This is an effect of grace. Many readers will be astonished to read the following sentence written by Claude Bernard, the great physiologist, whom his successors have tried to make out to be the doctrinaire of a rigorous and exclusive determinism of man: "Grace is necessary; that is to say, man is not free to change without it."

Yes, something must really change in the world, and this can come only through men who themselves are changed. But when a man is changed under the influence of grace, then not only the state of his soul, but also his whole comportment, is changed.

He is suddenly free from the old habits which kept him imprisoned, free from the rancor and remorse that consumed him, and is incapable of committing the injustices which formerly were his habit.

He also accepts the necessary sacrifices that go along with his faith. "There is no way of getting away from suffering without suffering," writes Dr. Stocker.[10] Society persecutes those who refuse to play its game. There will be businessmen who will become insolvent, teachers who will no longer be appreciated by their principals, artists who will forfeit their success, doctors who may not make a living, lawyers who will lose their clients, novelists who will no longer be able to pander to the taste of the crowd, politicians who will alienate the masses.

But this is the price that will have to be paid if any real change is to take place in history, if we are to have a new civilization in which the spiritual and the temporal are again united.

I do not, of course, identify this new civilization with the kingdom of God. I know very well that the eternal problem of sin will remain and that it will not be resolved until the end of time. Our great and only true hope is the triumphal return of Jesus Christ.

But what concerns us here is not the eternal problem but rather the historical problem, the problem of the particular crisis which the world has been passing through since the Renaissance. And just as the healing of Dr. Maeder's young patient was marked by the reawakening of his faith, so, I believe, our present crisis will be resolved through an "integration."

And the final return of Jesus Christ, which we await and expect because he promised it, will bring with it not only "a new heaven," but also "a new earth."[85] Even down to its final promises the Bible remains oriented upon the incarnation.

Hence if today we wish to cure the world of its neurosis of defiance, if we believe that this is possible, if we mean to put an end to the deep disharmony of modern life, if we are to help men become whole in a broken world, if we are seeking the way to a culture in which all the disciplines are inspired by God, we do so because he himself is calling us to this task. As in the days of the prophets his voice is raised above the ruins.

Notes: Works Cited

1. *Les grands appels de l'homme contemporain:* André George, "L'humanisme scientifique"; Henri Maldiney, "L'homme nietzschéen"; Pierre Hervé, "L'homme marxiste"; Gabriel Marcel, "L'existence et la liberté humaine chez J. P. Sartre"; Paul Archambault, "L'humanisme laïque, Gide, Valéry, Alain"; Father Boisselot, "Le chrétien." Paris, Editions du Temps présent, 1946.

2. Dr. Alphonse Maeder, *Ways to Psychic Health.* Trans. by Theodore Lit. New York, Charles Scribner's Sons, 1953.

3. Jean-Paul Sartre, *Existentialism.* Trans. by Philip Mairet; in *Existentialism from Dostoevsky to Sartre,* selected and introduced by Walter Kaufmann. New York, Meridian Books, 1956.

4. Wilhelm Röpke, *Le Problème allemand.* Lausanne, Payot, 1945.

5. Dr. René Allendy, *L'enfance méconnue.* Genève, Editions du Mont-Blanc, Coll. *"Action et Pensée,"* No. 2, 4th ed., 1946.

6. Dr. C. G. Jung, *"Werden die Seelen Frieden finden?"* Interview in *Weltwoche,* May 11, 1945.

7. Hilaire Theurillat, "Interview de M. André Malraux." Genève, *La Suisse,* December 20, 1946.

8. *L'avenir de la science:* Louis de Broglie, *L'avenir de la physique;* A. D. Sertillanges, *"Science et scientisme";* Raymond Charmet, *"Le mythe moderne de la science",* etc. Paris, Plon, Coll. *"Présences,"* 1941.

9. Dr. C. G. Jung, *Two Essays on Analytical Psychology.* Trans. by R. F. C. Hull. London, Routledge & Kegan Paul, 1953.

10. Dr. Arnold Stocker, *Le traitement moral des nerveux.* Genève, Editions du Rhône, 1945.

11. Dr. Jean de Rougemont, *Vie du corps et vie de l'esprit.* Lyons, Paul Derain, 1945.

12. Dr. Josef Gander, *"Die Entwicklung der Medizin von Virchow zu Tournier"* in *Civitas,* Vol. I, No. 9, 1947.

13. Dr. Henri Baruk, *Psychiatrie morale experimentale, individuelle et sociale.* Paris, Presses universitaires de France, 1945.

14. Dr. Roger Reyss, *"Les asiles de fous"* in *Le Semeur,* November, 1946.

15. Ch. Durand-Pallot, *Biologie et bonheur conjugal.* Neuchâtel, Delachaux et Niestlé, 1946.

16. Werner Kaegi, *"Le chrétien et les grands problèmes de droit du temps présent,"* at a conference in Zurich, May 12, 1943.

17. Jean Rostand, *La vie et ses problèmes.* Paris, Flammarion, 1939.

18. Gustave Thibon, *Diagnostics.* Paris, Librairie de Médicis, 1940.

19. René Gillouin, *Problèmes français, problèmes humains.* Genève, Editions du Milieu du Monde, 1944.

20. Henri Bergson, *The Two Sources of Morality and Religion,* Trans. by R. Ashley Audra and Cloudesley Brereton. New York, Henry Holt and Company, 1935.

21. Emile Bréhier, *Histoire de la philosophie.* Paris, Alcan, 1938.

22. Dr. Noël Fiessinger, *Le raisonnement en médecine.* Paris, Vigot, 1945.

23. Dr. Arnault Tzanck, *La Conscience créatrice.* Algiers, Charlot, 1943.

24. Théodule Ribot, *Les maladies de la personnalité.* Paris, 1914.

25. Dr. Henri Mentha, *"A propos de médecine psychosomatique"* in *Revue médicale de la Suisse romande.* Lausanne (June 25, 1947), p. 386.

26. Dr. Viktor von Weizsäcker, *Arzt und Kranker.* Leipzig, Koehler und Amelang, 1941.

27. Dr. Alexis Carrel, *Man, the Unknown.* New York, Harper & Row, 1935.

28. Ad. Ferrière, *Le progrès spirituel.* Genève, Editions Forum, 1927.

29. Leia, *Le symbolisme des contes de fées.* Genève, Editions du Mont-Blanc, Coll. *"Action et Pensée,"* 1943.

30. Dr. Paul Dubois, *The Psychic Treatment of Nervous Disorders.* Trans. and edited by S. E. Jelliffe and W. A. White. New York and London, Funk and Wagnalls, 1908.

31. Franck Abauzit, *L'énigme du monde et sa solution selon Charles Secrétan.* Neuchâtel et Paris, Delachaux et Niestlé, 1938.

32. Lecomte du Noüy, *L'avenir de L'esprit*. Paris, Gallimard, 1947.

33. Dr. Arnold Stocker, *Désarroi de l'homme moderne*. Genève, Editions du Mont-Blanc, Coll. "*Action et Pensée*," 1946.

34. Théophile Spoerri, "*La politique du Confédéré*" in *La Suisse forge son destin*. Neuchâtel, Editions de La Baconnière, 1942.

35. Dr. Marcel Sendrail, "*L'homme et ses maladies*" in *Revue des Deux Mondes*. Paris (Royat), January 15, 1943.

36. E. Boinet, *Les doctrines médicales*. Paris, Flammarion.

37. Roland Dalbiez, *Psychoanalytical Method and the Doctrine of Freud*. Trans. by T. F. Lindsay. London, Longmans, Green & Co., 1941.

38. Dr. Pierre Ponsoye, *L'Esprit. force biologique fondamentale*. Montpellier, Causse, Graille et Castelnau, 1942.

39. Dr. Arnault Tzanck, *Immunité, intolerance, biophylaxie*. Paris, Masson, 1932.

40. Dr. Georges Menkès, *Médecine sans frontières*. Genève et Annemasse, Editions du Mont-Blanc, Coll. "*Action et Pensée*," 1945.

41. Dr. Philippe Kressmann, *Humanisme médical contemporain et recherche d'une médecine chrétienne*. Bordeaux, Impr. Castera, 1945.

42. Dr. Agostino Maltarello, "*Spiritualità del medico*" in *Tabor*. Rome (April, 1947), p. 64.

43. Dr. Joseph Zwiebel, *Juif, parce que chrétien*. Paris, S.P.B., 1947.

44. Dr. Georges Liengme, *Pour apprendre à mieux vivre*. Neuchâtel, Attinger, 1930.

45. L. D. Weatherhead, *Psychology, Religion and Healing*. Nashville, Abingdon Press, 1951.

46. Henri Ochsenbein, *Les compagnons de la vie*. Strasbourg, Oberlin, 1946.

47. Dr. Pierre Delore, *Introduction à la médecine de l'homme en santé et de l'homme malade*. Paris, Masson, 1944.

48. Roger Schütz, *Introduction à la vie communautaire*. Genève, Labor et Fides; Paris, Je Sers, 1944.

49. Dr. Charles Odier, *Les deux sources, consciente et inconsciente, de la vie morale*, Neuchâtel, La Baconnière, 1943.

50. René Lalive d'Epinay, Théo Spoerri, *et al.*, *Pouvoir et travail*. Neuchâtel, La Baconnière, 1944.

51. Canon Fernand Boillat, *La société au service de la personne*, St-Maurice, Edit. de l'Oeuvre de saint Augustin, 1945.

52. Jacques Ellul, Paul Tournier, René Gillouin, *L'homme mesure de toute chose*. Genève, publication du Centre protestant d'études, 1947.

53. Edouard Burnier, *La maison du potier*. Lausanne, F. Roth, 1944.

54. Quoted by Dr. Gustave Roussy, "*L'avenir de la science*." Paris, Presse médicale, October 14, 1943.

55. Dr. Henri Flournoy, "*Un cas de psychopathologie*" in *Archives des sciences physiques et naturelles* (May–June, 1944), p. 67.

56. Ernest Renan, *L'avenir de la science*. Paris, Calmann-Lévy, 1934.

57. Henri Poincaré, *La science et l'hypothèse*. Paris, Flammarion, 1920.

58. Georges Salet and Louis Lafont, *L'évolution regressive*. Paris, Aux éditions franciscaines, 1943.

59. Charles-Eugène Guye, *L'évolution physico-chimique*. Paris, Hermann, 1942.

60. André Gide, *The Immoralist*. Trans. by Dorothy Bussy. New York, Alfred A. Knopf, 1954.

61. Dr. Arnold Stocker, *L'amour interdit: Trois anges sur la route de Sodome*. Genève, Editions du Mont-Blanc, Coll. "*Action et Pensée*," 1943.

62. Henri Bergson, *Allocution au tricentenaire du "Discours sur la méthode*," 1937.

63. Dr. Guy Trolliet, *L'évolutionnisme spiritualiste*. Bordeaux, Delmas, 1946.

64. Dr. M. Engelson, *L'homme dans l'espace et dans le temps*. Genève, Editions du Mont-Blanc, 1942.

65. Maurice Caullery, *Le problème de l'évolution*. Paris, Payot, 1931.

66. C. Depéret, *Les transformations du monde animal*. Paris, Flammarion, 1929.

67. L. Cuénot, "*L'adaptation chez les animaux*" in *Bulletin Soc. des sciences de Nancy*, No. 9., December, 1937.

68. Henri Bergson, *Creative Evolution*. Trans. by Arthur Mitchell. New York, Henry Holt and Company, 1911.

69. P. Lemoine, *Encyclopédie française*. Paris, 1937.

70. Y. Delage, *L'hérédité et les grands problèmes de la biologie générale,* 1903.

71. G. Montandon, *L'homme préhistorique et les préhumains.* Paris, Payot, 1943.

72. M. Boule, *Les hommes fossiles.* Paris, Masson, 1921.

73. Dr. Gustave Roussy, *Le vain secret.* Paris, Presse médicale, February, 1944.

74. Romans 8:20–23.

75. Max Picard, *L'homme du néant.* Neuchâtel, Editions de La Baconnière, 1945.

76. Dr. René Allendy, *Journal d'un médecin malade.* Paris, Denoël, 1944.

77. Charles Baudouin, *La force en nous.* Genève et Annemasse, Editions du Mont-Blanc, 1942.

78. Arthur Koestler, *Darkness at Noon.* Trans. by Daphne Hardy. New York, Modern Library, 1941.

79. Dr. R. Leriche, *Thromboses artérielles.* Paris, Masson, 1944; cited in *Revue médicale de la Suisse romande,* March 23, 1947.

80. Pierre Bouvier, *Sur l'interaction du rayonnement avec la matière en théorie de champs quantifiés.* Genève, Impr. A. Kundig, 1947.

81. Matthew 8:11.

82. John 1:46.

83. Dr. Jean de Rougemont, *Culture et misère humaine.* Lyons, Impr. Nouvelle Lyonnaise.

84. Dr. Edouard Schweizer, *"Jésus-Christ maître de la maladie et de la mort"* in *Le Semeur* (November, 1946), p. 15.

85. Revelation 21:1.

86. G. de Reynold, *Conscience de la Suisse.* Neuchâtel, Editions de La Baconnière, 1939.

Index of Names and Subjects

Abauzit, Franck, 33
Abrami, 45
Accident, 101, 102, 104, 105, 117f.
Adolescence, 2, 3, 4, 5, 8, 32, 84, 126
Adultery, 18, 21, 27
Aggressiveness, 15, 24, 25, 70, 73, 133
Allendy, René, 9, 34, 44, 45, 131f.
Ambivalence, 12, 13, 16, 17
Antiquity, 2, 3, 4
Anxiety, 8, 22, 88
Aquinas, Thomas, 52, 101
Archambault, Paul, 86
Art, 2, 24, 29, 32, 83
Atheism, 34, 77, 87, 90, 92
Atomic bomb, 9, 25, 83, 134
Augustine, 101
Authority, 3, 6

Bad Boll, 53, 162, 163, 167
Balzac, Honoré de, 123
Barth, Karl, 155
Baruk, Henri, 14ff., 18, 24, 40, 43, 45, 46, 50, 57, 58, 68, 69, 70, 73, 79, 83, 133
Baudouin, Charles, 136
Bergson, Henri, 25, 82, 91, 107, 114, 115, 123, 147, 149
Bernard, Claude, 38, 169
Bikini, 10, 135
Biology, 59, 82
Birth control, 18
Bohr, Niels, 82
Boillat, Fernand, 72
Boisselot, 93
Boule, M., 112
Bouvier, Pierre, 146

Bréhier, Emile, 26
Broglie, Louis de, 83, 135
Brunschwicg, 142
Buchenwald, 9
Buisson, M. F., 19
Burnier, Edouard, 79

Cabanis, 40
Capitalism, 20, 130
Carrel, Alexis, 29, 42, 122
Catholic Action, 165
Caullery, Maurice, 103, 104, 108
Charmet, Raymond, 142
Chesterton, G. K., 72
Childhood, 2, 3, 5, 13, 77
Church, 3, 17, 19, 22, 53, 76, 77ff., 81, 85, 89, 92, 94, 141, 144ff.
Cohn, 45
Communism, 20, 36, 87, 90, 129, 157
Complementarity, principle of, 82
Condorcet, Marquis de, 99
Conscience, 12ff., 17, 18, 22, 73, 84, 86, 102, 133, 135
Creation, 102, 110, 123, 143
Cross, the, 31
Cuénot, L., 106

Dalbiez, Roland, 40, 41
Darwin, Charles, 99ff., 108, 114, 118ff., 125, 129
Death, fear of, 12, 23, 93
Delage, Y., 108
Delore, Pierre, 65
Depéret, C., 103, 104
d'Epinay, René Lalive, 72

Descartes, René, 15, 16, 42, 75, 77, 80, 91, 99, 100
d'Estienne, Jean, 110
Diagnosis, 144f.
Divorce, 27
Dogmatism, religious, 34
Dostoevski, Fyodor, 19
Dubois, Eugene, 112f.
Dubois, Paul, 33, 40, 41
Durand-Pallot, Ch., 17, 18

Economics, 11, 24, 75, 85, 126, 142
Ecumenical Institute, Bossey, 154, 163f.
Eddington, Arthur S., 82
Egalitarianism, 130
Ehrlich, Paul, 38
Ellul, Jacques, 72, 91, 157, 167
Engelson, M., 102
Esquirol, Jean Etienne, 16
Euthanasia, 21
Evangelical Academies, 162ff.
Evil, riddle of, 121
Evolution, 97 ff.
Existentialism, 22, 87, 90

Faith, 76, 80, 84, 88
Fall, the, 33
Fear, 25, 137, 143
Ferrière, Ad., 30
Fiessinger, Noël, 26
Finalism, 105ff., 115
Flournoy, Henri, 80
Forgiveness, 129
Francis of Assisi, 143
Freedom, 87
Freud, Freudianism, 11, 14, 22, 24, 25, 40, 41, 46, 66, 86, 87, 88, 90, 92, 147

Galileo, 16, 81
Gander, Josef, 11
George, André, 10, 83, 135
Gide, André, 10, 23, 33, 51, 86, 88
Gillouin, René, 23, 92, 127, 136
Goebbels, Joseph, 9
Goethe, J. W., 152
Gosset, 65

Grace, 22, 169
Guilt, guilt feeling, 14, 15, 22, 131, 133
Guitry, Sacha, 18
Guye, Charles-Eugène, 81, 82

Haeckel, Ernest, 112
Hate, 69, 70
Hegel, G. W. F., 86
Heisenberg, Werner, 81
Heraclitus, 33
Hervé, Pierre, 30, 87, 129, 130, 157
History, 20, 87, 99, 166
Hitler, Adolf, 127, 161
Holy Spirit, 156, 159, 168
Hrdlicka, Ales, 112
Huxley, Thomas, 100

Incarnation, 160, 170
Indeterminacy, principle of, 81
Individualism, 22, 131, 157
Inferiority feelings, 131, 142
Inner conflict, 10, 11, 21, 25, 32, 77
Integration, 5, 170

John XXIII, 144
Jolowicz, Ernest, 14
Jung, C. G., 9ff., 22, 140, 141, 148
Justification by faith, 91

Kaegi, Werner, 19, 72
Kant, Immanuel, 28
Koestler, Arthur, 138
Kressmann, Philippe, 45, 64
Kütemeyer, Wilhelm, 53

Lafont, Louis, 103, 113, 115, 116, 123
"Laicism", 19, 34
Law, 2, 19, 20, 22, 24, 27
Leia, 31
Lemoine, P., 107
Leriche, R., 146, 166
Liberalism, 36, 85, 93, 119
Liengme, George, 57
Loeb, Jacques, 42

Loneliness, 9, 12
Loyola, Ignatius, 155

Maeder, Alphonse, 5, 6, 10, 11, 13, 24, 46, 73, 123, 133, 149, 150, 152, 154, 169
Maldiney, Henri, 127
Malraux, André, 9, 15, 24
Maltarello, Agostino, 49, 63, 66, 67, 89
Manuel, Eugène, 91
Marcel, Gabriel, 4, 10, 87
Marriage, 21
Marx, Karl, 24, 86, 88, 155
Marxism, 20, 92, 119, 127, 130, 155, 166
Masses, the, 137f., 160
Materialism, 36, 40, 41, 42, 90, 92, 101, 157, 166
Medicine, 2, 20, 22, 24, 33, 38, 41, 64, 66, 89, 122, 161, 162
Menkès, Georges, 44, 45, 121, 147
Mentha, Henri, 28, 40, 48, 63, 64, 66
Middle Ages, 3, 4, 16, 25, 74, 128, 152, 156
Monnier, 36
Montaigne, Michel de, 26, 27
Montandon, G., 111, 113
Moral consciousness, 11, 68
Morality, 11, 17, 22, 25, 82, 84, 86, 126, 159
Moréas, 91
Mounier, Emmanuel, 72
Mutation, 102
Mythology, 29ff.

Naegeli, Karl Wilhelm, 105
Natural selection, 100, 102, 105, 119
Nazism, 9, 33, 86, 90, 92, 121, 127, 135, 140f., 155, 162, 163
Neighbor, 55
Neurosis, 8, 9, 11, 12, 57, 61, 148
Neurosis of defiance, 5
Nietzsche, Friedrich, 4, 22, 24, 33, 34, 86, 88, 121, 126, 127, 155, 157
Nizan, Paul, 93
Noüy, Lecomte de, 33, 106, 108, 118, 147, 149

Objective knowledge, 22, 54, 76, 84
Ochsenbein, Henri, 63, 157
Odier, Charles, 66, 88

Paleontology, 96, 100, 103, 104, 110
Pascal, Blaise, 2, 13, 25, 49, 51, 135, 143
Pasteur, Louis, 39, 80
Pastoral care, 7
Paul VI, 144
Pavlov, 11, 41
Péguy, Charles, 142, 157, 160
Personhood, person, 36ff., 71, 73, 128, 168
Philosophy, 25, 26ff., 30, 75, 84, 108, 117, 119, 147
Physics, 81, 82
Physiology, 40
Piaget, Jean, 30
Picard, Max, 127
Pius IX, 143
Poetry, 2, 10, 25, 29ff., 75, 76, 88, 147
Poincaré, Henri, 80
Pokrovsky, 20
Politics, 11, 18, 24, 34, 85, 126, 138, 142
Ponsoye, Pierre, 42, 49, 53, 60, 61, 62, 65, 67, 82
Positivism, 82, 99
Power, myth of, 12. 95, 125ff.
Prodigal, parable of, 7
Progress, myth of, 33, 86, 95, 96ff., 125, 135
Projection, 13
Propaganda, 139ff.
Psychoanalysis, 13, 21, 33, 34, 41, 88, 91, 92
Psychology, 5, 26, 28, 40, 78, 132
Psychotherapy, 28

Raguin, 114
Reason, 16, 26
Reconciliation, 22
Reformers, the, 152
Renaissance, 4, 5, 10, 12, 25, 36, 56, 84, 86, 88, 128
Renan, Ernest, 26, 80, 91, 99

Repression, 12ff., 32ff., 50, 57, 84, 108
Revelation, 10, 97
Reymond, Arnold, 26
Reynold, G. de, 36
Reyss, Roger, 15, 46, 48
Ribot, Théodule, 28
Roch, 146
Röpke, Wilhelm, 9
Rops, Daniel, 72
Rostand, Jean, 104, 106, 165
Rougemont, Jean de, 11, 31, 43, 49, 53, 55, 56, 58, 65, 73, 79, 121, 128, 155
Rousseau, Jean-Jacques, 24, 92
Roussy, Gustave, 121

Sales, Francis de, 52
Salet, Georges, 103, 113, 115, 116, 123
Sartre, Jean-Paul, 4, 5, 8, 10, 19, 24, 25, 33, 85ff., 90, 123, 127, 155
Schütz, Robert, 65
Schweizer, Edouard, 166
Science, 2, 11, 12, 20, 23, 26, 28ff., 33, 66, 67, 69, 71, 75, 76, 80ff., 101, 109, 136, 142, 147, 160
Secrétan, Charles, 158
Sectarianism, 34
Sendrail, Marcel, 38, 39
Sexuality, 7, 18
Sin, 12, 22
Sin, original, 56
Skepticism, 33, 34, 77, 90, 123
Speransky, 44
Spiritualism, 33
Spoerri, Théophile, 36, 137
Stekel, Wilhelm, 13
Stocker, Arnold, 11, 12, 14, 36, 49, 51ff., 57ff., 71, 72, 169
Stoicism, 93

Struggle, 101, 102, 117ff., 125
Symbol, 29ff.

Taine, Hippolyte, 91
Technology, 11, 25, 33, 67, 75, 76, 121, 136, 160
Teilhard de Chardin, Pierre, 97ff.
Telepathy, 33
Theology, 27, 54, 78
Therapy, 144f.
Thibon, Gustave, 23, 88
't Hooft, Visser, 154
Totalitarianism, 22
Transformism, 97, 102, 104ff., 120
Trélat, 14
Trolliet, Guy, 101, 102, 110
Trousseau, 48
Tzanck, Arnault, 27, 43, 44, 59, 82, 104, 106, 140, 147

Unconscious, 10, 11, 29, 41
Urey, Harold, 25

Valéry, Paul, 9, 51
Vinet, Alexander, 143
Virchow, R., 38
Volney, Constantin, 99
Vries, Hugo de, 105

Weatherhead, Leslie, 57
Weismann, August, 105
Weizsäcker, Viktor von, 28, 62, 148
Work, 137
World Council of Churches, 144

Zwiebel, Joseph, 54, 75, 152, 153, 159